CASHLESS SOCIETY 101

CASHLESS SOCIETY 101

A Practical (Values to Action)
Guide to Ethical Leadership
and Inclusive Innovation

Brian Asingia

NEW DEGREE PRESS
COPYRIGHT © 2021 BRIAN ASINGIA
All rights reserved.

CASHLESS SOCIETY 101
A Practical (Values to Action) Guide to Ethical Leadership and Inclusive Innovation

ISBN
978-1-63730-666-6   *Paperback*
978-1-63730-755-7   *Kindle Ebook*
978-1-63730-869-1   *Digital Ebook*

To my love and family:

The world is yours and dreams do come true.

Trust Culture,

Asingia.

CONTENTS

INTRODUCTION	FROM VALUES TO ACTION	11
CHAPTER 1	FROM STRANGE FRUIT TO STREAMED LYNCHINGS	19
CHAPTER 2	ETHICAL LEADERSHIP IS TIMELESS	31
CHAPTER 3	CASH IS KING AND GREED IS GOOD	43
CHAPTER 4	CASHLESS SOCIETY AS A PHILOSOPHY AND DIGITAL ECOSYSTEM	55
CHAPTER 5	IDENTITY IN A CASHLESS SOCIETY	65
CHAPTER 6	OWNERSHIP IN A CASHLESS SOCIETY	77
CHAPTER 7	TRUST IN A CASHLESS SOCIETY	89
CHAPTER 8	SCALE IN A CASHLESS SOCIETY	103
CHAPTER 9	THE POWER OF INDIVIDUAL AGENCY AND ACTIVISM	117
CHAPTER 10	THE POWER OF SHARED VALUE	131
CHAPTER 11	THE POWER OF SHARED RESPONSIBILITY	149
	ACKNOWLEDGMENTS	163
	APPENDIX	165

"Society often forgives the criminal; it never forgives the dreamer. The beautiful sterile emotions that art excites in us are hateful in its eyes, and so completely are people dominated by the tyranny of this dreadful social ideal that they are always coming shamelessly up to one at Private Views and other places that are open to the general public, and saying in a loud stentorian voice, 'What are you doing?' whereas 'What are you thinking?' is the only question that any single civilized being should ever be allowed to whisper to another. They mean well, no doubt, these honest, beaming folks. Perhaps that is the reason why they are so excessively tedious. But someone should teach them that while, in the opinion of society, Contemplation is the gravest sin of which any citizen can be guilty, in the opinion of the highest culture it is the proper occupation of man."

—OSCAR WILDE (IN PRAISE OF DISOBEDIENCE)

INTRODUCTION

FROM VALUES TO ACTION

"It is not knowledge we lack. What we lack is the courage to understand what we know and draw conclusions."

—SVANT

"A racist feels their beliefs are just as right as an activist and that is our ultimate human dilemma, as we lack a shared set of values to agree on and embed in AI systems," Ernst & Young Ethical AI Advisory Board member Reid Backman, PhD, shared with me at the start of his interview for this book.

His comments mirror those of Dr. Annegret Berne, a German expert lawyer for labor law, who reminds me "the road to hell is paved with good intentions if you look at the religious Crusades to current technology…Humanity has not changed behaviorally in the last centuries since the colonialism and mass slavery eras, often extending groupthink and white supremacy ideology devoid of cultural relevance and localization." Our COVID-19 reaction, for example, was driven by fear and a short-term fix of policy mandates devoid of long-term testing or research such as masks mandates, initially unapproved vaccines, and costly lockdowns without ample testing of their long-term impact on individuals' health and rights. COVID-19 has shown the clear lack of ethics in defining both policy and equity distribution of vaccines locally and globally.

There is no doubt the business world has become the business of ethics. *The Wall Street Journal* states engaging on social issues is now part of the CEO job description but cautions it's a treacherous path. CEOs "put themselves on this path" by responsively engaging in social issues with their employees and partly as a form of marketing, says Harris Diamond, former chief executive of ad giant McCann Worldgroup, adding, "Once you open up that door, you have to live by it."

The proliferation of ethics and inclusive innovation debates in organizations are nothing new but are certainly trends here to stay. People are getting hired in technology companies without the proper or timely training to understand the ethical and valuable transfer consequences of the increasingly complex and automated systems they design and operate. *The Wall Street Journal* reported in April 2021 if Apple is King Kong and Facebook is Godzilla, mom-and-pop online merchants are worried they're the screaming, scattering citizens who are about to get stomped as these two giants battle it out.

Looking at BigTech firms like Apple and Facebook, the last few decades have lost trust through the terms "Too *Big* to Fail," "Fake News," "Misinformation," and "Deep Fakes," among other Internet-worthy memes. For example, Tate Ryan-Mosley writes for *The Technology Review* beauty filters are changing the way young girls see themselves, and the most widespread use of augmented reality isn't in gaming: it's the face filters on social media resulting in mass experiments on girls and young women that will show how technology changes the way we form our identities, represent ourselves, and relate to others.

In this book, I examine the ethical positions of people from various walks of life. Barack Obama places faith in America and the American dream through his book, *A Promised Land*. MIT professor, AI expert, and innovator Dr. Lex Fridman uses his Lex Fridman podcast to engage his peers and the scientific geniuses of our time across disciplines from AI to physics to psychology and philosophy. These conversations seek to answer complex questions about the ethics or effectiveness of artificial general intelligence (AGI), or the nerdy, "Is our humanity a simulation for another intelligent species?"

Evaluating the ethical leadership from tech companies in the last decade seems devoid of hope. I personally believe most universities are underequipped to handle the talent demands of the future. In fact, EdTech start-ups and tech corporations are stepping in with certifications programs, e.g., Google, Amazon, and Microsoft. Hence, ethical leadership experience and project-based learning will play a critical role in training the next generation.

This book is my attempt to help us understand how, both as a society and individuals, we can do better and fight for an ethical and inclusive future—a Cashless Society, with electronic payments or transactions and no cash transactions.

We need to do better because on top of a trustless digital ecosystem of "fake news" and "deep fakes" is a trend of creative destruction. Job losses from automation of low-, middle-, and even high-skill roles like stock picking leave a general fear of tech along racial and political lines. According to *Time*, Gabe Dalporto, the CEO of Udacity, which offers online courses in programming, data science, AI and more warn, "If you tried to reskill a billion people in the university system, you would break the university system." Despite the fact AI impacts everyone and is here to stay, "*No one is making sure the AI machines aren't racist*," reads a March 2021 *The New York Times* headline. "A billion people will lose their jobs over the next ten years due to AI, and if anything, COVID-19 has accelerated that by about nine years," says Dalporto.

My underlying thesis is technology is unbiased. Most people believe AI is a threat to human sustainability, agency, and control; humans would never design systems that betray humanity; and data privacy is irrelevant if one has nothing to hide. *But* based on my research and experiences, I think:

- AI, while neutral and not an end in itself, is influenced by the human values or lack thereof programmed and codified into it

- Humans increasingly learn, work, think, and act as a herd via groupthink

- Individual agency of ethical leadership and innovation based on shared values are critical to scale in a Cashless Society

Because humans create technology, we need to be skeptical of it and work to make it more effective, i.e., less biased. There is clearly a lot of work to do:

- The European Union (EU) does a conservative innovation and regulation model where "do no harm" is the norm, as seen by their Astrazeneca COVID-19 vaccine halts.

- The US is an "experiment and self-regulate later" nation.

- China offers clear innovation policy guidance via its multiyear plans for strategic industries and sectors such as the Belt and Road Initiative, i.e., Silk Road 2.0.

- The West takes other cultures and their contributions for granted while the rest of the world is fighting to decolonize innovation.

- Inclusive innovation is the best way to guarantee a Cashless Society accessible to all, e.g., mobile banking for the four billion of the unbanked.

Personal interest and curiosity about agency, ethics, and inclusive innovation are primarily why I am writing this book. My personal journey of growing up in Uganda helped me see the dark side of corruption firsthand. In August 2006, I resisted pressure to bribe a local Ugandan official to verify via stamp the residency documentation I already had. I grew up seeing my father endlessly scapegoated and jailed for bribery scandals performed by his superiors. As if that was not enough, I learned as a nine-year-old, my mother lost her job for resisting to honor unethical favors from her boss at school. I am curious about the role of ethical leadership and decision-making in a world or society that prefers and normalizes the easier and unethical way out.

This book is for:

- Youths in your twenties to thirties seeking to find your own moral compass beyond the historical and group-think religious, business, and political lenses of today

- An executive or emerging leader anxious about the unknown and how to lead or listen before acting through an ethical lens

- Those of us who value the power of individual agency and accountability despite social and institutional normalization of unethical and amoral policies and decisions with long-term implications

More importantly, this book is for those who wish and want to do better by questioning, asking, discussing, analyzing, and acting on the day-to-day challenges and moments of our generation. "Your life starts getting worse when you start advocating for underrepresented people," Dr. Timnit Gebru, an Ethiopian American computer scientist working on algorithmic bias and data mining, said in an email before her firing from Google's AI ethics team. *The New York Times* quoted her as saying, "You start making the other leaders upset."

You should read to understand:

- Cashless Society as a philosophy of frictionless—i.e., cashless values-based—exchange

- Cashless Society as an ideal technocratic realization with its pros and cons, i.e., technology is neutral, but humans are not

- Ethics- or values-based leadership and inclusive innovation in the Fourth Industrial Revolution

The book captures inspirational stories of ethical leadership and inclusive innovation through primary interviews with leading experts and scholars. One such story is Dr. Jose Morey, *Forbes* innovation expert, whose greatest accomplishment is founding Ad Astra Media to bring STEAM to students through space comics and animations that look like them, underpinning the increasing lack of identity representation in science and technology as well as media. Facebook Africa CEO **Nunu Ntshingila** asserts their belief everyone's story needs to be supported and shared. I also share personal stories, like when I quit a paid consulting project where the CEO was willingly ignoring anti-money laundering laws and guidelines in automating a FinTech product.

As you read *Cashless Society 101*, you will see the difference between what we fear about Cashless Society, "**used to describe a system in which people pay for things by using bank cards, moving money over the Internet, etc. rather than using cash in the form of coins and notes**" as defined in the *Cambridge Dictionary*, and how we can be active participants in realizing an ethically designed and inclusive digital ecosystem for all. In the 1950s, the "*Cashless* Society" was as much a part of an idealized modern future as the jetpack and the flying car, according to *The Atlantic*. This book redefines Cashless Society through an ethical lens to explore issues of identity, ownership, trust, and scale in a no-cash-transactions ecosystem as well as an ethics-first innovation society. This book is your practical guide to ethical leadership and inclusive innovation in a Cashless Society.

CHAPTER 1

FROM STRANGE FRUIT TO STREAMED LYNCHINGS

"The human race is a herd. Here we are, unique, eternal aspects of consciousness with an infinity of potential, and we have allowed ourselves to become an unthinking, unquestioning blob of conformity and uniformity. A herd. Once we concede to the herd mentality, we can be controlled and directed by a tiny few. And we are."

- DAVID ICKE

In the land of the free and the home of the brave (#ThisIsAmerica), technology has only extended or exposed the brutality of a police force against the very citizens it is supposed to protect and serve, as per the Hollywood famous Los Angeles Police Department (LAPD) Academy motto. For some, the system is working as intended, with police, militias, and racists continuing an age-old US tradition of hunting, lynching, and killing nonwhites. There lingers a part of the US population afraid the nonwhites will one day overpower the white population, as illustrated by demographic changes to be explored in further chapters. From the book *Guns, Germs, and Steel* by Jared Diamond, we learn in some cases where people have felt to be superior, they bully others just to "prove" their superiority. This inherently racist fear and/or superiority complex-driven agenda has had broad implications across the US and the world. It is worth reviewing how we got here and why technology (guns, body cameras, security cameras, or phone tracing) alone without the ethical human decisions and radical change is not the answer or end in and of itself.

Beyond policing, there is a broader implication of the abuse of technology for unethical purposes by both government and citizens. Technology is neutral and merely extends human values and actions. Slavery, colonialism, and their long-term setbacks for mankind are well documented across nonfiction and fiction, such as Joseph Conrad in his book *Heart of Darkness*, where he captures the rise of *white supremacy* in Europe. The white supremacy bug, like a virus or dangerous idea, spread by targeting civilized Jews, Muslims, Americans, and Africans before and up to the late fifteenth century, where colonialism, at its peak, caused human loss under the guise only the West is civilized. Here it is, just as important to note even the words "civilized" or "civilization" have historically been used as a tool of white supremacy, i.e., which societies are deemed "civilized" versus "uncivilized," and who makes that distinction especially in the colonial or imperial context. Today, it is under the development lens economically, e.g., China, US, or EU seeking to develop other countries or the religious lens spiritually and the spread of democracy or rule of law, also known as the political lens.

For example, even after colonialism, the so-called "free states," like the United States of America, mirrored Britain's prioritization of slaveowners and traders over the oppressed by financially compensating slaveowners for their sacrifice during abolition. Indeed, the US continues its Jim Crow era of segregation against African Americans, mass incarceration for free prison labor, low to impossible minimum and living wages for manufacturing, and low-skilled jobs mirroring China.

Neocolonialism through low- to no-cost value and resource extraction, such as economic policies by the World Bank, Britain's Commonwealth, or France's colonial tax on West African countries, rule the day. All this is legal in the so-called "civilized West" because they fundamentally devalue those different from them. One need not look further in time to see this, as one of the twenty-first-century leaders of the US, Donald J. Trump, states, "These aren't people, these are animals," in referencing immigrants from nonwhite countries, as reported in *The Washington Post*'s history of dehumanization in the US. This dangerous white supremacy idea of othering and dehumanizing is why freedom was offered for natives of the North Americas or Native (American) Indians, but slavery was reserved for so-called "savages and brutes," including the Africans.

This othering is happening again against a new species of work. Robots, here to replace humans in various jobs like construction via 3D printing of houses or even stock picking through algorithmic trading, are now the new other against which humanity seems to be rallying. Human fear of robots and digitization, including digital currency, is real. Thus, automation through creative destruction is replacing some jobs in a COVID-19 era of high unemployment and job scarcity. Unfortunately, the US, and in some ways global Western society, is copying by othering along racial lines where the "fragile white," as covered in the book *White Fragility*, feel threatened by the shifting demographic trends, with over 51 percent of newborn Americans now nonwhite, according to the 2020 US Census report. This predictable near-term reaction led by fear includes desperate measures such as pushing others into helplessness, submission, hiding, escape, suicide, resistance, assimilation, and demoralization as mostly white Americans try to validate their privilege to the limited jobs and opportunities of today.

I am reminded of a time in middle school (secondary school for Africans) when we read Chinua Achebe's novels—*Things Fall Apart* and its sister narrative, *No Longer at Ease*. The latter explores a young man's struggle to adapt to the expectations of his local culture after studying abroad, from marrying a woman from the caste (out of his tribe) to slowly being trapped into a cycle of bribes and corruption just to get his bearings in his new city job. The protagonist, Obi Okonkwo, studies in Britain and returns to work in colonial civil service, where he ends up taking a bribe, a turning point he never escapes. This character's journey has haunted me all my life.

To do better at trade than slavery—the original sin of capitalism (free labor)—civilization, not colonization or extermination, must rule the day. I do not advocate for the destructive western idea of civilization, for there is power in story and narrative, but the humanity-focused decolonial lens of civilization, "Ubuntu." Ubuntu, in Zulu, refers to oneness—"I am because you are." We can and should establish value inherent in each of us before some government, church, or monarch acknowledges us. The need for family, tribe, or nations to protect, fight, and die for each other must not be driven by racial hatred and the dehumanization of others.

"We don't have to talk about world leaders, because we already have world leadership in tech corporations like Apple and Microsoft, who we cannot live without if they shut down, and ignoring that fact and reality only makes things worse in the long term," says Dr. Annegret Berne, a German expert lawyer for labor law and colleague. She adds, "The road to hell is paved with good intentions, and if you look at the religious Crusades to current technology, humanity has not changed behaviorally in the last one hundred years." Anne doesn't see any point in turning around. She argues some minorities are becoming extreme and an opposition to the majority, "becoming righteous rather than having a broader society vision."

To Anne and many history observers out there, there is no recognition of the unethical structures because the picture does not come in black and white with clear symbols of meaning. For example, we are reacting to symptoms of COVID-19 and not the underlying issues of lack of transparent and ethical leadership or decision-making by humans. We often just react to a quick fix instead of a mid- to long-term survival strategy, unlike animals, which are way smarter and actually make decisions that would benefit their offspring, not just short-term survival. Even a bird creates a nest for her eggs and watches out for prey. Savannah animals like zebras or antelopes will signal via noise or other techniques when they are in danger of a predator like a lion to protect each other, especially the vulnerable young ones. The COVID-19 vaccine, masking resistance, unequal distribution, and access to healthcare, among other unethical policies, show the lack of shared concern for each other's welfare and health among humankind.

Anne rigorously concludes we are just changing scenes with the public consent just like in the Nazi era. In a way, argues Anne, "We as a society or public are complicit in this boring game of life and dictatorships." The silver lining in all this is the business world has become the business of ethics with increasing social demands on corporations to do the right thing as well as capitalism seeing environmentally, socially, and governance friendly corporations like Tesla win the day.

For example, according to WP Tavern, WordPress Themes Team rep Ari Stathopoulos reports on one of their 2021 internal change management meetings, "In the meeting, we discussed the need to change the review process." His team seems to agree: "All guidelines have a reason they exist. They were all added after some things got abused. But the process followed had an unfortunate side effect; the rules that were added to avoid abuse by a few bad apples are the same rules that hinder innovation and deter people from submitting a theme in the repository."

He brought up the universal rules of not doing evil things, disrespecting others, or abusing the system, citing them as the foundation of what the guidelines should be. He adds, "But then, of course, everyone has a different definition of evil, disrespect, and abuse, so something a bit more verbose may be needed, but obviously not as verbose as the dozens upon dozens of guidelines we currently have."

Automattic, the company behind the free, open-source, and premium versions of WordPress, provides a sustainable model for the future of open, decentralized, and collaborative innovation that is no longer 100 percent proprietary (private or confidential) and siloed. Similarly, Sun Microsystems, the company behind Red Hat Linux and creator of Java prior to their Oracle acquisition, is a leader in open source. The Oracle vs. Google case with Oracle suing Google for using part of its Java (Sun Microsystems, the owner, was acquired by Oracle) code as part of the Android operating system of the 2010s was recently ruled on in 2021 by the US Supreme Court in favor of Google's fair use of code argument as reported by NPR in April 2021. The Oracle vs. Google ownership argument, now reshaped as Apple (closed data access) vs. Facebook (open data access) in 2021, underscores the ethical concerns of ownership of innovation, code, and/or design in a Cashless Society.

Ownership, like any value or concept, varies by culture or geography and is often complicated when we factor in historical and political lenses. One example is looted art exclusively commercialized in prestigious museums around the world, often under the guise of safeguarding it from ruin by the very people who created or inherited it. Ideas, and by extension intellectual property, from copyright to patents and trademarks have a similar history of being stolen, misappropriated, and commercialized, degrees away from the original or "rightful" owners, from Ford's controversial "stealing" of the windshield wiper idea to American pharmaceutical companies registering and monopolizing AIDs medicine at the expense of Indian and other global medical innovations. Recently, there has been a rise in patent trolls or troll culture making its way to the highest office in the land—the US Supreme Court. The US-China trade disputes—as detailed by China-US briefings and IP bans against TikTok, Huawei, and others—show how there is often confusion and a lack of clarity around ownership and the rights to trade or commercialize IP across the world.

The World Intellectual Property Organization (WIPO) and other regional intellectual property (IP) offices across the US, Europe, China, the Americas, and Africa—such as the African Regional Intellectual Property Organization (ARIPO)—claim to provide clarity and frameworks for registration and commercialization of IP but are often limited in both their rulings. These rulings are often in favor of corporate or individual trolls against single owners or small company innovators, as was the case for Cheek'd dating app. The Cheek'd patent troll lawsuit, even if ruled in favor or against the patent troll, was a damages case that took four years and delayed *Shark Tank* entrepreneur Lori Cheek's business, as reported by IPWatchdog.

PriceEconomics.com reports in the US, there are numerous examples of copyright being extended rather than expiring as per original statutes to favor reigning commercial enterprises like Disney, Hollywood Studios, and others. Thus, for the US, a country synonymous with "private property rights," the playing field is far from fair due to the assumed global domain of US IP; as such, it makes the international arena even more challenging when it comes to both compliance and enforcement of policies. It is no wonder the US is surprised by China and India's recent push to register, own, protect, and commercialize more of their IP both locally and globally.

China currently leads the world in new global IP patent registrations, according to the World Intellectual Property Office (WIPO) 2020 Report, which states China's IP office received 1.4 million patent applications in 2019, more than twice the amount received by authorities in the second-busiest country, the United States (621,453). The China-US trade war being fought via an IP proxy and the court of public opinion are clear indicators of the copycat culture of China's post-cultural revolution era, as illustrated in *China in Ten Words*. This copy culture has evolved and matured into a full-on global innovation strategy. China is not only playing by the rules of IP registration and enforcement but also winning at innovation, such as their 5G and now 6G wireless technologies.

China's digital innovation success often redefines the global trade and soft power rules to the US and EU's frustration. The US, despite its deregulated—and often self-regulation preferred—environment, feels threatened by China because it is the Chinese state directing China's innovation via its long-term strategic agenda. This wave of global resistance—from China to India and now Africa—against mass import and expansion of US technologies and conglomerates highlights the growing politicization of innovation and, in particular, the historical context of extractive innovation in colonial and post-colonial times.

Britain's Navy, printing press, and ultimately the Bible, with millions of copies printed, gave it unparalleled control of the sea, media, and ultimately colony minds, ensuring a complete yet "diplomatic" control of its territories for both trade and resource extraction. For Britain and other "Great Seven" countries, or G7, human plus intellectual capital and natural resources were obtained at near zero to monopoly pricing via its royal charters and recently one-sided trade agreements.

The US, a self-declared leader of the "Free World," is just as guilty of exploitative tactics. America has and continues to invest in securing military might, mass surveillance, and communications tools, as well as critical "goodwill" via its embassies and physical presence in almost every major country and/or landmass. The pattern is thus one of might is right, and unfortunately, as the Cashless Society becomes a reality, economic control becomes a critical status symbol. The US economic leadership is close to being lost to China due to China's increasing influence globally in both military as well as "goodwill" efforts. China, through development aid and strategic initiatives like the "Silk Road Initiative," also known as the Belt Road, is connecting major ports and cities by infrastructure investments in ports, rails, and other related projects such as 5G and soon 6G communications technology to power this Cashless Society. For America, often prioritizing oil and the military, digital and indeed intellectual property warfare is a tie to a near loss should it continue down the "US first and US only" route.

The Cashless Society is decentralized despite global superpowers' push to regulate, control, and tax every facet of this transition. Because of the existence of all types of implementations in both the foundation infrastructure such as 5G, or 6G for China, or the underlying technology like blockchain, there are varied design choices from centralized servers to decentralized nodes and a combination of hybrid architectures. Thus, mass adoption is being realized across different implementations, from digital to mobile to wallets to debit cards to phone and off-chain (off-network) storage devices. Consumer adoption and use of cashless systems, such as buying cars and houses in credit cards or crypto, is becoming the inevitable norm. This is contrary to earlier speculation and calls for crypto bans by the US federal government and other global governments. For example, China, as of 2021, is regulating mining of major cryptos, as well as almost normalizing its digital reserve currency, ahead of other major global central banking institutions. China is poised to lead global market adoption of digital reserve currencies and, with it, almost strategically render the US dollar irrelevant in the long term.

A common perception among emerging markets like Africa is the International Monetary Fund (IMF), alongside the World Bank, is designed to keep Africa in perpetual poverty.

> *"If the owners of the natural resources go around begging, then you should know there's something wrong with their minds."*
>
> - PRESIDENT PAUL KAGAME.

Kagame also shared with *The Africa Report*, "Africa has been struggling to follow the West, and now that system is crumbling." The tech and financial changes discussed earlier are critical to moving toward the Cashless Society. My earlier points about racism and colonialism's impacts are reduced if there is decentralization in finance, hence more local ownership and involvement, such as Guatemala's recent move to bitcoin as a national currency and China's digital federal reserve currency plans. The same can be said of a thriving mobile money ecosystem, M-PESA, in East Africa that is processing billions of dollars in value daily through a simple local SMS-based innovation independent of global financial systems. This bottoms-up, decentralized, autonomous innovation is both a means of resistance to colonial and racially biased design and an engine for local inclusive innovation that scales across cultures and borders. I advocate for a move toward digital and mobile service delivery beyond just cryptocurrency over cash. This move, which includes electronic transactions, eliminates bureaucratic paper waste, improves transparency as well as makes innovations more accessible locally without requiring a western or neocolonial approval, thus helping address these systemic problems of exclusive innovation, lack of local ownership, and minimal scale.

CHAPTER 2

ETHICAL LEADERSHIP IS TIMELESS

"We increasingly rely on data we do not trust."
- THE PRINCIPAL POST CEO
[PHONE INTERVIEW APRIL 2021]

When I once used the US as an example of good diplomacy in a friendly discussion, my Senegalese colleague corrected me by clarifying there is a difference between soft power diplomacy and bullying, and the US was the latter. The US, despite its moral ground, has been a participant in methods of genocide: massacre; CIA-linked assassinations, e.g., Patrice Lumumba of the Democratic Republic of the Congo; sterilization, e.g., Latin America; mutilation; destruction of cultural symbols, e.g., Middle East; deportation; starvation, e.g., Southern Border; forceful conversion, e.g., anti-Muslim rhetoric; separation of families, e.g., under Trump; and its original sin, slavery. This is best captured in the White House-screened racism propaganda film *The Birth of a Nation* that also gave rise to the racially biased Hollywood of today, as captured by NPR in its one-hundred-year retrospection on the film. "I just think the way it's taught is more important than the fact it's taught," says Todd Boyd, a professor at the University of Southern California's School of Cinematic Arts, who has stopped using it to teach film school in California, USA. Boyd, who is the Katherine and Frank Price Endowed Chair for the Study of Race and Popular Culture at USC, adds, "If you talk about it only as technological achievement and the brilliance of D. W. Griffith, then I think it is unfortunate. If you talk about it as representative of racism, white supremacy, and America's history in this regard, then I think that's very different."

The social implications are such that immigrants must hate or look down on nonwhite immigrants or descendants of slaves, Native Indians, and Mexicans to appeal to white privilege in an almost forced assimilation culture that adopts poor whites, the Irish, Italians, Jews, Latinos, and now some "model minority" Asians to keep the "white supremacy" ideology alive. Ideally, freedom, justice, and service should be accessible to all, and part of the challenge for our generation and the task is to not sweep this under the rug but face it head on. I use the US to highlight how a self-declared moral and ethical leader of the world falls short on their promise even at home and leaves a leadership vacuum with dangerous consequences for unethical values and innovations. Any hindrance to a critical exploration of ethics, civilities, and/or other liberties in the US and the world is a threat to justice and inclusion everywhere and ultimately only seeks to protect the status quo that is power based on a white supremacist ideology. There are meaningful guiding principles such as "equal justice under the law" and "the pursuit of happiness" to American idealism, as enshrined in the US Constitution, that ought to be accessible and applicable to all, not just a few. As the US is grounded on private ownership, private citizen rights, and/or personal liberties, it is necessary private enterprise be the sector through which meaningful advocacy and change occur as a compliment to the existing legal, political, and/or religious avenues. In other words, private actions and private enterprise can and does have a history of being part of the problem of racism, exclusion, and inequality and should not be isolated or protected from criticism or meaningful change toward a more ethical and inclusive society.

For example, the investment communities' push for geopolitics to pivot and put critical issues of our time front and center is a striking indicator of the ESG investment phenomenon where environment, social, and governance are core factors in determining the investment in a company. Increasingly, we are seeing what I call the "conscious consumer movement" grow. Consumers want to know the carbon footprint of their food, clothes, and transport, as well as the ethical sourcing, manufacturing, and data policies behind the brands they love or engage with. As such ethical brands stand to gain in the long term as the cancel culture, #MeToo, and #BLM (Black Lives Matter) movements increase social and economic accountability for unethical and exclusive leadership or innovation. In particular, for the digital transaction-driven Cashless Society, companies like Facebook, Apple, Amazon, Netflix, Google (Alphabet), and Microsoft are being put through this ESG lens. Companies like Tesla, pushing for a greener planet through electrification of our ecosystem and an ideally solar-powered transport network, are winning.

We have moved from *who killed the electric car* to *who does not want an electric car*, thanks to the genius of Elon Musk and his entrepreneurial leadership.

However, while Tesla may do well through the environment, social, and governance (ESG) lens, a company can be good in some ways (environmental, for example) while having issues in other ways (exploiting workers or suppressing unions). Thus, I advocate for giving credit where credit is due while still challenging brand and leadership where there is room for improvement instead of blind or absolute morality expectations and/or loyalty in today's cancel culture. It is not just me or popular comedian Dave Chappelle who are rallying against cancel culture. According to *Politico*, both presidents Barack Obama and Donald Trump agree with the majority of Americans that cancel culture is not as effective or productive alone and should be complemented with actual work to mitigate the issues of our time without reducing civil liberties.

According to BlueAndGreenTomorrow.com, entrepreneurs and investors are leading an activist-driven path to tackle the world's biggest challenges, such as climate change, where politicians have failed. One such agenda is Morocco's aggressive investments in solar and renewable energy across Africa while the West continues to rely on fossil fuels or oil. Across the world, from wind energy in Kenya and solar in Morocco, India, and China, the world is no longer waiting for the West to lead. Rather, there seems to be a strategic resistance building to the "West is Right" or "Might is Right" mindset and instead channeling innovation to local challenges with global potential. Granted the green revolution will take a while, these strategic investments in solar across Africa, where the Sun's position is an added advantage, create meaningful foundations of a reliable energy source critical to the inclusive Cashless Society we all need. Across the globe, there is an increasing sense that despite the hype, the EU and US could be holding global innovation hostage, as seen by their recent hesitancy to openly approve sharing COVID-19 vaccine manufacturing rights to other companies in other countries.

The old world of US- and EU-first patent and IP registrations is being countered through local IP protection and enforcement against foreign brands such as Apple's loss of the iPhone trademark to a Chinese leather goods brand, according to Reuters. The World Economic Forum analyses this decolonization is consistent across the BRICS (Brazil, Russia, India, China, and South Africa) and soon across Africa and Asia with governments focused on nurturing and protecting local innovations from foreign competitors. Having learned from the cash- and debt-driven World Bank development policies of the twentieth century in Africa and the Caribbean that were almost always economic and social disasters, albeit for some good PR of loan forgiveness, the new leadership in these countries understands too well the myth the West is always right and resists implementing development agendas based on the West's prescription.

From forming BRICS banking and informal trade affiliations to other regional trade associations, the global market is being organized to counter the often cartel-like coordination between Europe on behalf of her former colonies and the US on behalf of her territories. By strategically moving from cash-focused innovation to an ownership-driven agenda, BRICS, and soon most emerging countries like Kenya, are understanding the value of ownership in a Cashless Society in solving local needs and meeting international demands, according to Capacity Media. For example, it is reported Joe Mucheru, Kenya's ICT cabinet secretary, has given the country's foreign-owned firms a deadline of March 2024 to ensure 30 percent local ownership (equity ownership). This is a trend shared more and more across Africa from Ghana to South Africa, from Senegal to Ethiopia and Rwanda, in line with the African Union Agenda 2030 and 2063.

There is a realization excluded communities have inherent value, and it is not the IMF or World Bank alone that has keys, let alone solutions, to economic and social mobility. States are tapping into innovative hybrid models that leverage mostly human and intellectual capital via technological innovations backed by financial capital. This hybrid model guarantees local innovators ownership, or at least state ownership. Thus, the cheap or near discounted transfer of IP to foreign conglomerates and/or governments, as is often the case with British, American, and French institutions, is under check. Driven \to own more, control more, and earn more, innovators across the world, backed by their local government's favorable policies, are giving Western firms a run for their money. TechCrunch reported in 2016 Netflix was still struggling to capture more than 1 percent of the African subscription market. This lower market share is due to a lack of local and authentic culturally responsive media, as reported by AllAfrica news syndicator Nextv Africa. According to Yahoo!, Amazon had no choice but to partner with local Indian production firms and studios to deliver culturally relevant media. TechCrunch also reports Google, Facebook, Amazon, and Apple are no strangers to the "difficulty of doing business" in China or India, as they claim. This is actually due to identical, if not better, existing local services that put cultural relevance and localization first and hence capture the local market.

By assuming the digital and mobile-first Cashless Society user will only speak English, French, or other romance languages, Western firms have excluded and in return missed out on the next generation of Internet users. In the digitized Cashless Society, non-English- or French-speaking users from emerging markets will be part of the global nonwhite majority that values culture and local relevance above all else. From Africa to Latin America and Asia, there is increasing demand for cultural representation in media, technology innovations, and, yes, even boardrooms. Supportive governments like China, Rwanda, India, and Kenya, among others, are already drafting and implementing local ownership laws that protect their citizens' innovations from investor shacks who often buy IP for peanuts and short-change the local innovators.

The Wall Street Journal, TechCrunch, *The Verge*, *The Times of India*, Reuters, *Quartz*, and *Fortune* all agree Indians are realizing and asking, "Why should America, and by extension, the West, have all the fun?" Local innovations are gaining social and political support to scale in critical categories like digital payments, e-commerce, data, healthcare, and education. Indian conglomerate Reliance Industries Limited, for example, has partnerships with Facebook and Google to develop FinTech in India. The global trend, it seems, is decolonization. Decolonization in innovation means less direct technology transfer of importing from the west and more strategic and equal partners collaboration to scale locally developed solutions that compete with western innovations. With increased local, state, and innovator ownership, more revenue, tax revenue, and even global brand or state credibility is possible, as seen in China, Kenya, Rwanda, and now India when it comes to digital payments. According to philosopher and society commentator Bertrand Russell, collective fear stimulates herd instinct and tends to produce ferocity toward those who are not regarded as members of the herd.

While I argue technology is neutral, it is an expression of our values and ways of doing things. The cautionary tale against technology starts with an exploration of human nature, which is riddled with mistakes and biases against "others" different from them. A critical look at US history reveals "Manifest Destiny," or the US westward expansionist self-determinism, is but a clean or blurry version for "Exterminate all the Brutes" where it is not just about guns, steel, and germs, but the elimination of others, i.e., the first Americans via the Indian Removal Act, medical experiments on African Americans, and anti-non-white immigrant propaganda. According to History.com, Manifest Destiny, a phrase coined in 1845, is the idea the United States is destined—by God, its advocates believed—to expand its dominion and spread democracy and capitalism across the entire North American continent. It is also shared the philosophy drove nineteenth-century US territorial expansion and was used to justify the forced removal of Native Americans and other groups from their homes. These white supremacy-driven genocides, left unchecked, empower genocidists with responsibility, intent, motivation, feelings of guilt, and a demoralization campaign against others, often including the use of technology to achieve such unethical but surprisingly legal (slavery, Jim Crow, and voter suppression were/are legal) agendas.

Similarly, Big Tech, especially in the US, remains unchecked. According to *MIT Technology Review*, Facebook's ad algorithms are still excluding women from seeing jobs. Reporter Karen Hao claims Facebook's ad delivery system is excluding women from opportunities without regard to their qualifications, a process that would be illegal under US employment law. The audit, conducted by independent researchers at the University of Southern California (USC), reveals Facebook's ad delivery system shows different job ads to women and men even though the jobs require the same qualifications. *The Wall Street Journal* reported in April 2021 if Apple is King Kong and Facebook is Godzilla, mom-and-pop online merchants are worried they're the screaming, scattering citizens who are about to get stomped as these two giants battle it out. The proliferation of ethics and inclusive innovation debates in organizations is nothing new, but it is certainly a trend here to stay.

Historically, a lack of ethical leadership is at the root of limited trust across institutions today. Treaties meant acceptance of other nations, so violations of Indian treaties followed in the birth of white America with slavery as a necessary evil. Genocide won over coexistence, as shared in the Home Box Office (HBO) series *Exterminate All the Brutes*. The docuseries argues the aftermath is still felt today with global cultural losses, dislocation, moral deterioration, political changes due to imperialist, and ethical leadership vacuums globally. Before the nuclear disasters, government surveillance, and job losses due to automation, there were unethical human values being prioritized over ethical values. Our task, it seems, is to first explore ethical values, especially shared values, and then act radically and meaningfully toward a digitized or electronic Cashless Society of ethical leadership and inclusive innovation.

In an interview with Principal Post founder Bruce Taub, he told me, "We increasingly rely on data we do not trust." Ethical leadership and inclusive innovation are the answers to our electronic transactions Cashless Society dystopia that increasingly widens the gap digitally and economically between the rich and poor, as well as along racial, sexual, and political lines. In the US, for example, Coca-Cola and Delta received blowback from both the pro-civil rights left and the pro-business right for their flip-flop (initially pro- and later against the law) response to Georgia's new voting law, SB 202, which extends voter suppression measures targeting black and minority communities, such as limited mail-in voting, according to *The Wall Street Journal*.

Data, AI, and society nonprofit member Jacob Silverman capture the uncertain terrain of ethical AI with Big Tech links to unethical tech use in his *The New Republic* articles. A year into his investigation of ethical AI at Big Tech firms, he reports it's clear basically nothing has changed. He argues many tech companies still maintain contracts with law enforcement agencies and a US military engaged in a disastrous forever-war. According to Jacob, despite the occasional charitable donation or burst of progressive rhetoric, these tech companies remain aligned with institutional power and the violence through which it's maintained. *The New York Times* and other major journals like NPR have reported extensively on a court case involving Apple refusing to turn over some data from two phones first in 2016 and recently in 2020 to the FBI, where the court subpoena was denied and the FBI had to resort to private security consultants to unlock the device. NPR reports the logic behind Apple's public refusal: "Under well-settled law, computer code is treated as speech within the meaning of the First Amendment," Apple says.

Facebook is unfortunately guilty of handing over troves of data to law enforcement, especially after the heightened racial tensions in the US, allowing both prosecutors and the police to target people of color speaking out against police brutality. *The Guardian* shares that Robert Peralta, a 35-year-old activist and musician, didn't think twice about his 23 January Facebook thread criticizing the police until two months later, when he learned that police had issued a warrant for his arrest – accusing him of threatening to kill law enforcement. His felony criminal case is part of what civil rights campaigners say is a disturbing trend of police and prosecutors targeting activists for social media posts, arresting users over innocuous political messages that constitute free speech.

"For a country that purports to be guided by democracy and civil rights, this is a very dangerous and slippery slope...Black activists are expressing anger, rage, and hatred even about the conditions that threaten their daily lives, and they are being held liable for how they express that anger, even though they've committed no crime."

- MALKIA CYRIL, THE EXECUTIVE DIRECTOR OF THE CENTER FOR MEDIA JUSTICE IN THE GUARDIAN.

"None of this is exactly revelatory, but identifying the deep connections between Big Tech and the carceral state is a necessary part of the project of dismantling those things. You can't really see the whole of one, at this point, without looking at the other."

- JACOB SILVERMAN, THE NEW REPUBLIC.

Thus, the age-old statement "guns don't kill people, people do" holds for now, until automated guns or machines become the norm and change the rules of the game. Humanity—both through unethical leadership from CEOs like Facebook's Mark Zuckerberg and exclusive innovation of companies like Apple—is at the core of the challenges and opportunities for change for our generation, not technology or the threat of robots.

CHAPTER 3

CASH IS KING AND GREED IS GOOD

"Technology has changed a lot since 1996. Shouldn't Internet regulations change too?"
— @WSJ.COM FACEBOOK AD 3/20/2021 10:33 A.M. EST

As I research for this book, a Facebook ad on *The Wall Street Journal* catches my eye, and yes, we can assume it's targeted to me and others similar in profile with the brave acknowledgment of Facebook's support for a change in Internet regulations since 1996. Of important concern is Facebook is a US company with other subsidiaries in Africa, Ireland, and other locations, as reported by *The Irish Times*. The ad speaks to Facebook's recent controversial growth amidst political misinformation and racial tensions almost at the expense of human rights. Facebook is not alone; in fact, it can be argued the world is in competition to claim the evilest company. Whereas Facebook sees 1996 as an important milestone for reflection, I would push us all to look further into human history, for as a species, we are quick to forget.

The British Empire and other colonial expansion models later adapted by the US and now China offer no room for human rights. Rather, multinationals subsidized by governments offer a technocentric and almost authoritarian industrial complex that extracts more than it sustains or creates and commercializes more than it rewards. In short, humanity, like in the slavery era, is the product and/or commodity that must be sacrificed or maximized at the behest of a few humans. This human sacrifice now includes rights and exclusive legal protections for company boards, corporations legally termed "persons" in the US, and most areas.

Corporations, like colonial royal franchises, provide adequate abstraction and protection from any legal and/or ethical obligation by the individuals overseeing them. This corporate oversight by boards of directors, managers, and/or executives is shielded through the inherent corporate structure, insurance as well as other public relations mechanisms. This remote extraction of value from human capital and institutional operation at a distance from communities leaves the fate of humanity and future generations to robots or artificial lifeforms who can easily replicate these management roles. One may ask why the protected rich would want to turn their cushy, responsibility-free positions on the board of directors over to robots and AI? The answer is automation in a lot of roles is inevitable, as seen in fund management with robots outperforming human financial managers. For leadership, there is the allure of delegating decision-making and/or business process and oversight to robots either to allow for more productivity but also to further shield the person from any risk since the board is liable in some special circumstances where fraud, negligence, and other crimes are committed.

As if this is not enough, we rely on a third-grade literate political elite, a policy council often decades behind in regulating innovation. The average congressman, senate member, or politician panders to the social gullibility with little regard to the understanding of technology innovations like the Internet, blockchain, and artificial general intelligence. One need not be torn between agreeing lawmakers don't understand technology and thinking they understand it perfectly and are intentionally choosing not to regulate it for their own reasons. Both situations exist concurrently where leaders often legislate from ignorance or lack of urgency until things go wrong, then they often don't act due to lack of political will or conflicts of interest from financial incentives like inside trading of stocks and lobby or campaign contributions. After all, cash is king and greed is good in the land of the free and home of the brave.

When I was a junior at Lafayette College in Pennsylvania, USA, I got introduced to policy as part of my electives and interdisciplinary studies, where we explored the process for a piece of legislation to become law and the different branches of government. The US has three main branches of government, each with different roles. The actual ramifications of the separation of powers among the executive, legislative, and judiciary are often lengthy but mostly lawful. This lawfulness, however, should not be misinterpreted as ethical; as the US history can testify, legal does not always mean ethical if we look at slavery, Jim Crow, anti-abortion, banks denying real estate loans from certain communities, and countless other legal but unethical practices. I was amazed at how complex the US legislation machine is, and rightfully so. Checks and balances come with a price, and there is a long history of the

US delivering that legal, moral, and ethical compass for its citizens and the world.

However, one could argue America, with its War on (foreign) Terror manages to turn a blind eye to its homegrown gun violence and terrorism. Likewise, its "war on drugs" focuses on other countries while ignoring addictions and a racialized drug business at home. Its pseudo-democracy export to other nations in exchange for those very countries' wealth and resources has failed, and its self-declared "world police" role is devoid of exemplary ethical leadership over many decades. Perhaps we all need an adult conversation on how we got here, with leadership filled with hypocritical or conflicting duality, and what we can each do about it. I still have faith in humanity, particularly individual accountability over abstract corporate and/or institutional changes often decades behind innovation.

We need not forget why the United Nations was formed after World War II, a war that involved and affected mostly Europe yet involved the world's resources due to the interlinked extraction-based industrialization, or the Universal Declaration of Human Rights. To most excluded nations in emerging markets, such as Rwanda, as articulated by former African Union chair Paul Kagame to Reuters, this is because the UN is largely led by representatives from expansionist countries like the US and Britain. To date, there is no permanent member country on the UN security council from Africa, a region with over 1.3 billion people critical to global security and economic sustainability. One could argue civil rights, women's rights, and LGBTQ rights, among other movements, are an evolution and response to the brutality and inhumanity of

absolute capitalism or inhumane and unethical innovation. The royal, empire-like, expansionist mindset that has troubled all major civilizations from Egypt to Rome, from Great Britain to the Soviet Union, and from America to China all point to a lack of international understanding and collaboration. Lack of ethical, equal treatment of all human beings across public and private institutions is the root cause of the pressing issues of our generation. All this is on a backdrop of growing impatience with the UN and its failure to lead ethically. The imperialist-driven UN security council is often enforcing superpower- and security council member-friendly policies against the weak in warzones, the vulnerable like Palestine, and emerging markets like Africa.

The cycle seems to be tremendous losses of lives, racial and economic disparities, and near collapse of civilizations or social orders toward a better society. So, to dream of and realize a sustainable Cashless Society, one has to acknowledge or define to what end the society aspires. I argue a Cashless Society ought to be a philosophical aspiration of humanity first, human values-based innovations and leadership, and ultimately, a technocratic realization of that dream. Thus, technology, to me, is a tool for progress toward a better society. Identity through social, cultural, and economic representation plays a big part in that. Yet, at the peak of our twenty-first century, humanity still struggles to meet her basic needs, let alone define her core values. Breakthroughs from artificial intelligence to gene editing to space exploration and intergenerational connectivity via the Internet of Things leave an increasing digital divide among countries, especially between the rich and the poor. What do we fundamentally, as a human race, aspire or wish to embed in the machines or artificial reflections we create? We seem to be in disagreement here. As such, we are failing to even agree to principle ethical standards and values that can be embedded in a foundational AI layer and inspire future ethical innovations.

On 3/17/2021, 6:31 a.m., *The Wall Street Journal* (*The WSJ*) reported, "China's new digital currency Is easy to use, but you'll be watched." *The WSJ* adds as China moves closer to rolling out its new digital cash, there are concerns the government will track every transaction—not just of citizens but of foreign companies in the country. The concern for government interference in day-to-day citizen interactions and experiences is one of the reasons against an electronic transaction-driven Cashless Society. Ironically, the cash or bureaucratic paper backlogs used today is neither decentralized nor trust-proof in that it is issued often by a central bank or government for the sole purpose of control via taxation as well as being open to counterfeiting among other challenges like physical damage and loss. The risk in a Cash Society seems to be ignored perhaps because it is the status quo; thus, the resistance is against the change toward a digitized or, even better, a tokenized ecosystem.

For starters, beyond complex stock, debt-equity derivatives, sophisticated accounting, and/or financial engineering to create wealth from existing assets, the average citizen looks toward extracting value via service or production delivery, not accounting and financial engineering. As such, the argument against government tracking is almost moot since cash, at least via banks and other mechanisms, is already tracked. The government already tracks large cash transactions, so people who obtain a lot of money in sublegal ways need to launder it. With a digital or electronic system, banking records are easily accessible for compliance, and even peer-to-peer transactions come with a level of trust within a friends and family circle, making these systems more reliable as they leave a digital trail when needed. The exception, of course, is the anonymous or identity-free decentralized finance platforms such as in the crypto space, but these should not be the only means of transaction.

This is not to disregard the steps most wealthy estates and corporations go through to avoid taxation and other declarations, just like small businesses, such as most restaurants and/or laundry businesses that may prefer a "Cash Only" policy. For most, the ability to "cook" the books and under-declare earnings for tax purposes as well as inflate cash flow and/or assets when it's time for loan applications or other critical transactions are worth fighting for a Cash Society. These concerns, ironically, are the very arguments raised against a Cashless Society, with most arguing cryptocurrencies like bitcoin and Ethereum on decentralized exchanges and non-identifiable wallets often leave result in a lack of ownership and responsible transactions and is likely to lead to fraud and illegal transactions such as the famous "Silk" exchange lawsuits and subpoenas against drug trafficking with crypto. While this is the exception and not the norm, illegal transactions beyond government and centralized control are the very reason licenses and mass adoption of a Cashless Society starting with crypto has been slow and fragmented.

I have experienced both worlds, a Cash Society in Uganda until I was eighteen and a digitized Cashless Society over the last fifteen years in the US. Within the US, I intentionally minimized and almost eliminated cash transactions. Given my experience is both worlds, I will never advocate for a Cash Society only. Perhaps that's the early adopter in me. The reality is the images, one of Zimbabweans with worthless or inflated currency notes in wheelbarrows and trash bags to make daily shopping errands vs. the second image of a Kenyan with their text-based mobile money transactions across borders. This binary dichotomy leaves the choice clear if aesthetics and simplicity alone were the deciding factors. Unfortunately, that is not the case.

In most countries like Uganda, my country of birth, the government, often a dictatorship, is in the business of money rather than providing welfare and services to their citizens. According to Monitor and CNN, the Uganda government's priority seems to be taxing their citizens and future revenue to incentivize citizens to find work or money, all in a country where unemployment is often 40 to 70 percent for recent youth and college graduates as per the World Bank human capital report. This is on top of a country with little to no financial literacy from the citizens to the government officers. For example, members of parliament found it wise to add a digital transactions tax on mobile money transfers and social media data fees without understanding the negative impact of added cost barriers to local and cross-border trade or e-commerce. This high cost of financial flows leaves me hoping for a rapid acceleration and adoption of decentralized finance and open banking solutions over the Cash Society.

Looking at the almost undisputed increase in small to medium enterprises (SMEs) and mobile money (MoMo) banking, the implications of a Cashless Society are clearly in favor of digital, inclusive, and decentralized open banking, especially for the four-billion-plus who are still unbanked globally. Analyzing entrepreneurship across East Africa compared to West, Central, or South Africa, one can see this validated in favor of digitization. Mobile banking is thriving in East Africa, such as Kenya, due to favorable government policy and staggering in other regions, like Nigeria, where there is limited support for open digital or mobile banking in favor of a Cash Society powered by traditional and exclusive banks rather than open and inclusive telecoms.

Thus, the issue of ownership starts from the very nexus of capital and, in particular, ownership to the means of access, transaction, and/or savings/investments. Government alone cannot deliver sufficient liquidity, volume, and dynamic market-driven incentives to sustain a society. At the extreme, a decentralized framework delivers the most impact with hybrid centralized vs. decentralized infrastructure coming second and the centralized Cash Society third when access, inclusion, and social economic impact and cross-border trade are factored in. To understand this fully, I shall use my personal experience with both the Cash and digitized Cashless Societies in the United States (US) and extend the philosophical and design limitations with the US. This US critique, despite their good intentions, contrasts the friends and family experiences I hear from across the world. To me, sending money to families at home is still a hustle, yet local mobile payments have made it easier for Ugandans to pay for utilities and government services like taxes and fees, a contrast to an often bank-tied cash system in the US.

America, despite its ideals, resists facing its original sins: slavery and racism. As such, it innovates on top of a deeply biased and racialized system without adapting to an equitable reality within its very constitution. Generalizations or observations aside, one need only show up at their bank to apply for a loan and see how they're treated compared to their white colleague or apply for a job in a historically "red zone," something I have personally experienced. *The New York Times* recently ran a report on code switching at work and the long-term impacts of red zone policies in banking where certain demographics were racially excluded from service based on their zip code, a practice that still affects credit history and generation wealth transfers such as home ownership.

The same applies to buying a new home, running for office, or even voting by ballot, evidenced in the 2020 election results rejection reaction by more than 40 percent of Americans storming the US capital, according to Statista. This racial and historical bias proliferated decades of education, health, housing, and banking or financial data from credit scores, the blood of American finance to home and business ownership, the soul of the American dream. They say those who live in glass houses should not cast stones, and America would be wise to look inward rather than externally when criticizing, let alone influencing, global financial innovations and commerce. The entrepreneurs and powers that be are already pushing toward financial and economic independence and inclusion without the US.

I fundamentally believe digitizing processes and currency is critical as it leads to more cost savings, up to 80 percent, as reported by the *Financial Times*. The report also mentions transparency via real-time or third-party reporting and/or verification in the case of blockchain. Surprisingly, despite the myth digital banking or decentralized finance leads to more fraud/illegal behavior, Cashless Society actually allows for more effective anti-money laundering, anti-theft and anti-corruption policy innovations, and enforcement compared to limited or untraceable cash. So, while some of us are pro-progress, we all need to think more about digital innovation, automation, and a Cashless Society. This is all due to its historical, current, and future ethical and economic implications that impact us all directly and indirectly in the short and long term. These implications are discussed in the rest of the book, starting with the role of identity, ownership, trust, and scale in a digitized Cashless Society. Most importantly, the Cashless Society conversation is explored through an ethical leadership and inclusive innovation lens.

CHAPTER 4

CASHLESS SOCIETY AS A PHILOSOPHY AND DIGITAL ECOSYSTEM

"We wanted to extend the Internet so it manages a computer platform."
— DOMINIC WILLIAMS, DFINITY FOUNDATION FOUNDER AND CHIEF SCIENTIST ON BLOOMBERG TV.

Janet Yellen, the 2021 United States Secretary of the Treasury, in one of her first tweet storms, shared a note on the turning point in global "monetary and fiscal" policy and, by extension, geopolitics:

"The first objective is a stable and growing world economy that benefits the US economy. For the United States to prosper, our neighbors, too, must prosper. Strong and stable economies abroad make us safer. And as we pursue a stronger world economy, we must also pay attention to existing financial stability risks and new risks that may arise. The second objective is to fight poverty and promote a more inclusive global economy that aligns with our values. Current crises will push almost 150 million into extreme poverty this year, reversing trends of the last two decades, with women, youth, low-skilled, and informal workers hard hit. We need to help lessen economic pain in low-income countries during a protracted recovery period and use this opportunity to facilitate structural transformation to more inclusive, sustainable economies. Our response will not be successful if we end up just where we were before."

- @SECYELLEN

For Janet and other practical realists, the old world order is gone and a new era is upon us. The new era, like any blank page or canvas for a writer or artist, is an opportunity to right the wrongs of the past and rewrite the rules of the game based on our shared human values. For what is progress without bettering our best? In echoing her @SecYellen tweet series—"our response will not be successful if we end up just where we were before"—Janet calls on Americans and ethical leaders globally to seize the moment and act not just for their citizens but for their neighbors as well. For what good is capitalism and free markets if there is no one to trade with?

The US and its currency, the dollar's, hold and facilitation of global markets since World War II is nearing its end if business continues as usual due to changing external factors like digital banking innovations and a global awakening to the self-serving US dollar policy that often excludes the critical needs of other countries, especially emerging markets. A strong US dollar is not necessarily good for emerging markets, yet most policies with long-term global implications are based on the US dollar or forced to due to its liquidity facilitation role in international trade and commerce. A rise in China and other BRICS member countries, like India, as well as emerging marketing innovations, like mobile banking across Africa, threaten this hold on large economic and political influence for the US.

While we are not likely to see major changes in the next decade due to slow and unclear digital banking regulatory policy globally, the tide is already changing with China's rollout of its Digital Reserve Currency and the era of the US dollar as the global standard is blurring. So rather than deny this reality, pragmatic solutions and policies that are still US-focused but inclusive of emerging markets and US neighbors offer a more sustainable path toward a digitized Cashless Society for all, as urged by Yellen. In her words, "America first must never mean America alone…When it comes down to it, credibility abroad begins with credibility at home."

It is important to note Janet Yellen is not a fan of the bitcoin cryptocurrency and cautions against rapid or accelerated adoption of these alternative forms of payment and transactions, pushing instead for more anti-money laundering (AML) and know your customer (KYC) policies to strengthen a cash-based society. However, her acknowledgment of the limitations and rather exclusionary, not free market, role of the US dollar offers a foundation for both critical debate as well as inclusive policy design and implementation. Ultimately, the ideal is to bring the unbanked and traditionally underserved into the dream that is capitalism on steroids, a.k.a. the American way.

The historical lack of trust in the cash-based global financial system is no different from the inherent human fear and distrust of technological innovations, including digital banking. According to Kinsta.com, even open-source and remote collaborative projects like WP Themes by Automattic Inc. are facing trust issues internally. For context, Kinsta reports Automattic Inc. is the creator of WordPress, which powers over 65 percent of the Internet's content management systems (CMS) as of December 2021.

Their latest piece of the Plugins and Themes Change Management proposal introduces the concept of a yes/no voting mechanism for end-users. These would be "trust tags" that allowed users to mark themes as updated, visually broken, and more. The goal is to hand over much of the gatekeeping responsibility to users, putting them in the driver's seat of what they want out of the theme directory, adds the Kinsta report. The concept, also shared by Facebook and Apple, albeit to different stages of giving more users data privacy control, is becoming a commercializable trend, where individuals could even cash it on their private data usage, according to MarketPlace.org.

WordPress's commitment to improving trust among its users and community in its software, process, and solutions is an increasing challenge for both public and private sectors. From misinformation to digital fakes and exclusive design that often do not cater to cultural responsiveness, the Internet is becoming Americanized, racially and policy-wise, which is not necessarily a good thing for the world.

Most would argue only the US stands to deliver the digitized Cashless Society we deserve, not China, Africa with fifty-four countries, India, or other regions. I beg to differ, arguing instead for an inclusive, decentralized framework that leverages and builds upon trustful and trustless technologies like the Internet and blockchain as well as centralized (identity-based) vs. decentralized (nonidentity-based or anonymous) solutions. For example, the US dollar-based global policy, as stated by Janet Yellen, is due for an upgrade that could have lifelong and intergenerational implications for millions, if not billions, globally from the unbanked (about four billion) to those in emerging markets, as well as US neighbors.

If identity and ownership are critical pillars of ethical leadership and inclusive innovations, as explored in earlier chapters, then trust is the perceived reality and expectation from the citizens, community, and counterparties in a Cashless Society. Trust, for the sake of this discussion, can have various meanings, as we will see for governments, private sectors, and consumers. But in the end, it is trust, or lack thereof, that will swing the pendulum toward mass adoption of ethically designed and inclusively accessible digital innovations, especially financial technology (FinTech) and other emerging technologies for the fourth industrial revolution (Cashless Society).

"Garbage in equals garbage out" is an old programming and data science statement meaning corrupted information leads to biased or equally corrupt results, and this has never been truer than in the last decade and moving forward. Big data, the ability to generate, store, and analyze large datasets, has grown from a marketing catchphrase to upsell more software to a Cashless Society reality. Institutions from governments to private corporations and even nonprofits increasingly rely on data for their security, operations, and service delivery without pausing to ask if their data is reliable, let alone inclusive enough.

Such is the ethical dilemma in our world. Before e-commerce or real-time data-driven service delivery, there was no efficient and sustainable scale, meaning you only banked with your local bank or shopped from your neighbor or local store. Reliable and near real-time data powers scale across time zones and borders. Thus, we need to measure and analyze data to make scalable decisions such as when to open a cafe, launch a new bus route, or the old computer science problem of what is the fastest route from A to B applicable to package and/or food delivery companies. The underlying challenge of data-driven logistics has never been more paramount than during the COVID-19 pandemic. There has been ongoing research and debates on effective vaccine distribution plans and strategies with live data feeds on every major website updating near real-time with fatalities and vaccination efforts updates.

New York City, for example, an early adopter of open data and governance, has had its share of being blindsided by data. NYC relied on elderly housing data from the state issued by the governor's office to make policies that were later found insufficient due to doctored data from Governor Andrew Cuomo's office, who has since resigned on sexual harassment accusations. With lives on the line and ethical leadership vacuums everywhere, there have been data scandals globally. Florida, for example, refused to credit rogue data scientists' COVID-19 datasets to the Trump administration and, in the process, lowered the severity estimates of the pandemic. Data, as the old saying goes, is capable of telling us whatever and, in this case, anything we wish it to tell us.

As usual, the failure is human, not necessarily technology, underlying how far we have to go to restore trust in both science and technology as well as the data that powers our society. This is especially true and visible from stock markets that rely on high-volume order routing to Uber and other modern transportation that dynamically auctions or prices trips based on demand. Ultimately, even a healthcare system forced to digitize overnight to respond to a pandemic is not spared the data analysis at scale need. This seems to be the foundation of decision-making everywhere. New York City, one of the worst-hit cities in the world, relied on data (infection rates changes, vaccination rates, changes, and death rates among other datasets) to make short-term and long-term policy on hospital operations, public service delivery, transportation, school openings, and vaccination rollouts, among other mandates.

Despite this well-meaning use of data and the efforts, most states and institutions still fall short from an ethical perspective due to biased data and human error. Vaccine distribution, for example, ended up not being equitably distributed across the US across racial demographics in favor of whites, even when the data clearly showed minority neighborhoods and communities disproportionately impacted by COVID-19. Likewise, the Paycheck Protection Program (PPP) meant to support small businesses in retaining employees again ended up in the hands of large institutions, not the very small businesses and communities they claimed to help. This is in part due to American greed that prioritizes large organizations due to a historical racial bias from banks against communities of color who often get sidelined from loans and credit access, a pattern that remains unbroken centuries later, according to the 2021 White House report. To put this in perspective, the Biden administration had to enact a separate policy window targeting PPP just for minorities and small businesses, including freelancers, because they could not trust the system to implement the original policy mandate fairly. Such is the reality in America despite good intentions from the legislature and congress.

Trust or lack thereof is not just in government but in private institutions as well. DFINITY Foundation, the decentralized

Internet computer, founder Dominic Williams shares in a May 7 interview on Bloomberg TV, "The Internet computer works differently in that today, a lot of blockchains run on the cloud, but the Internet computer runs on nodes machines hosted by independent third parties around the world." He hopes this decentralized Internet computer will power websites, Internet services, and leverage tokenization (partial digital credit ownership of assets like real estate or utilities) on top of the Internet. DFINITY has received VC backing from Andreessen Horowitz, plus one hundred VC and hedge funds and before that, several hundred backers. DFINITY is part of the hype and actualization of the decentralized autonomous organizations (DAOs) frameworks and ecosystems that include Decentralized Finance (DeFi) for blockchain-based banking. The DAO concept is members buy (stake) partial ownership into a system and are custodians able to vote on key decisions based on the entities' founding rules, all via the Internet to trigger-automated smart contracts or code that executes to implement certain functionality such as releasing funds, paying a client, or even closing the entity. It becomes a form of automated authority or decision-making, but more accessible from traditional boardroom structures.

For blockchain and decentralization to scale to the masses, security, and/or trust, remains a top concern. On the Tech Bytes section on Bloomberg TV, Mark Fisher, Google director of product management, identity, and user security, shares, "Google envisions a password-free future—basically moving from signing in with password every time to using devices to securely authenticate." Google is set to require two-factor authentication (2FA) via chrome browser and Google's Android plus Chrome operating systems (OS).

> *"Do I wanna put all my eggs in one basket?... It's better to focus on the most protected area that is secure, and trends are that there are more and more attempts to hack systems and more for users and institutions to lose."*
>
> - MARK FISHER, GOOGLE DIRECTOR OF PRODUCT MANAGEMENT, IDENTITY, AND USER SECURITY.

However, for Google, help is on the way, and users can check their authentication security by accessing.co/securitycheckup. Mark ends with what every Internet user should know: "... We already didn't trust the network." Trust, it is clear, is the foundation for scale in a Cashless Society. It is no wonder Google is pledging ten billion US dollars to cybersecurity, according to a Bloomberg report. According to Gizmodo and my industry analysis, Apple, Facebook, Amazon, Microsoft, Huawei, and Samsung, among others, are already exploring a passwordless future where digital identities and/or biometric security is the norm and not the exception.

CHAPTER 5

IDENTITY IN A CASHLESS SOCIETY

> "An integrated, prosperous, and peaceful Africa driven by its own citizens and representing a dynamic force in the global arena."
> - AFRICAN UNION AGENDA 2063 VISION.

As of May 2021, M-PESA, the Safaricom Telecom-owned mobile banking service, is now global with Visa and other third-party support services like Flutterwave, linking PayPal's millions of customers to African merchants as reported in *Business Insider*. Betty Mwangi, a Kenyan female employee of Safaricom and the company's financial services general manager, understood the magnitude of the project in 2015 and the need for African data sovereignty and security as shared in detail in my first book, *The Last Digital Frontier*. She pushed for the server transfers from Germany to Kenya so Africa would have both data custody and legal jurisdiction to this trillion-dollar financial transfer ecosystem. Thus, on April 16, 2015, CoinTelegraph.com reported Safaricom customers were greeted with news they should prepare for a new mobile banking revolution after the shutdown servers were moved from Germany to Kenya. Mobile and digital payments are much bigger than the western perception of convenience or speed and provide banking and financial services to millions, soon billions traditionally unbanked, unlocking a new audience, market, and service delivery model that is mobile and digital.

In the last decade, we have seen a radical shift from traditional banking to digital and almost predominantly mobile banking accelerated in this decade by COVID-19 and the global need for contactless payments, which increased by 20 percent, according to a McKinsey & Company report. Already piloted and scaled in emerging markets like Kenya in East Africa and frontier markets China, Japan, and South Korea thanks to Ant Financial, Samsung, and Huawei, the digital revolution is the new norm in the US, also seen by peer-to-peer bank transfers via services like Venmo, PayPal, Cash App, and Zelle. This mass adoption is all thanks to Wall Street's hunger for high-performing technology stocks like e-commerce, FinTech, and cybersecurity sectors despite a rusty and sluggish banking sector that only innovates when pushed or challenged by upstarts like Square and PayPal.

There is no doubt a tech or telecommunications company turned mobile or digital bank like Safaricom or recently Airtel could grow to become more relevant and powerful than an entire country's banking system. Such was the case for China's digital upstart Ant Financial started by Alibaba's Jack Ma. The success of digital banking is so strong China is aggressively regulating and "moderating" private companies' influence in the finance and economic freedoms of the Chinese people, as evidenced by Jack Ma's silence and delayed Ant Financial IPO in China in 2020. Jack Ma caught the attention of the Chinese Communist Party (CCP) after advocating for more financial freedom for Chinese citizens outside the government's control. Not surprisingly, some top party leaders are already owners or stood to benefit from the Ant Financial public stock exchange listing. China's regulation of bitcoin mining, with a majority of miners residing in China, as well as its recent launch of a national digital currency despite resistance to other cryptocurrencies, like bitcoin and Ethereum, show its need for control and ultimately acknowledge the power and inevitability of a Cashless Society. As Jesus said, "Give unto Caesar what is Caesar's." Governments or governance will always exist in some shape or form, but they may not control all transactions, and that is the beauty of peer-to-peer decentralized or token-based transactions that support for value transfer and exchange and sometimes holding without triggering a taxable currency event depending on the digital currency regulations of the land.

Africa, like Asia, can no longer sit by and watch the rest of the world innovate thanks to the development and early scale of M-PESA, the first and most successful mobile money payments service, according to *Forbes*. Globally, M-PESA, from its early stages, was the largest mobile money network in the world. Africa has caught the eye of FinTech and innovation funds, large and small. That Africa is home to 1.3 billion people and the youngest youth population in the world is lost to most westerners, particularly Americans. The financial and economic potential of this resource-rich continent and its traditionally unbanked but increasingly Cashless Society is a case study on the need for more ethical leadership and inclusive innovations globally.

M-PESA in Kenya thrived, for example, due to the government's free market and innovation-friendly policies, whereas mobile money has stalled in West Africa, in particular Nigeria, due to lack of supportive governments and policy, such as the requirement of age-old cash banking licenses for anyone to operate a digital bank. The cash-based and backward policies of Nigeria, despite having the leading African Fintech innovators, is a major reason, while Nigerian founders and many entrepreneurs across Africa are registering their companies in the US first to gain credibility before expanding to Africa. Such was the case for Flutterwave and the recent Y Combinator company **Plexo** that had to incorporate in America to find the respect, credibility, and investor trust needed to operate and scale in the global financial remittances business.

In fact, the historical lack of trust and often unreasonably high fees charged by cash-based remittance ventures like MoneyGram or Western Union and the digital hybrid WorldRemit are the reason Africans—both young and old, male and female, small business and large institution—are embracing the Cashless Society, having been mostly unbanked under the cash-based society. While the majority of Africans are yet to experience cross-border mobile banking, they are already familiar with SIM card fees and/or airtime credits. These digital SIM credit refills, often gifted from relatives locally and abroad, are the foundation and basis for the globally successful digital banking and SMS money transfer and billing ecosystem perfected and scaled by Safaricom as M-PESA.

M-PESA is now in East African countries like Burundi, Kenya, Rwanda, Tanzania, Uganda, South Sudan, and Ethiopia and scaling across Africa and the world thanks to Visa, Flutterwave, and other global payment gateways and application programming interfaces (API). What should not be lost to the world is the M-PESA success despite the simplicity in design (SMS texting), near-perfect security (national phone registrations), and inclusive accessibility of M-PESA as every African has one or two feature phones on average. Across Africa, smartphones are increasing in penetration, now over 33 percent as of 2021 and projected 65 percent by 2025 as reported in the GSMA Report. The biggest hindrance to the adoption and scale of this simple, elegant African solution to centuries of extraction-based policies and financial exclusion is the politicians, or the people's government, as the corrupt like to be called publicly. Nigeria, in particular, just like South Africa, has failed in leading Africa despite both countries' large sizes and economic relevance. Instead, it is small but strategic countries like Kenya and recently Rwanda that are leveraging their citizens' voices, the youth innovation, and a decolonization push from the African diaspora. Rwanda and Kenya's presidents have mastered the political will, a rarity in Africa, to exercise ethical leadership and implement-free market and entrepreneur or innovation-friendly policies that foster open, connected, and inclusive innovations.

Beyond Kenya and Rwanda's push for local ownership and representation, Africa is leading the world in decolonizing education and innovation thanks to inspiration from China and, recently, India. The most recent is the COVID-19 Mauritius innovation from local herbs and its cashless knowledge share with the rest of Africa to keep COVID-19 mortality low despite western countries' disapproval as it lacked the "made by the West" stamp. Similarly, Morocco's solar revolution against fossil fuel imports, like the M-PESA revolution, seeks to power Africa's next innovations, one with power and the other with capital. Libya's leader Muammar Gaddafi's dream of a united Africa with its own gold-backed single currency may be far from fruition, especially after the US unilaterally killed him without any plan and left the country open to more chaos than it was in before, a signature US Foreign Policy move just like the CIA assassination of DRC's Patrice Lumumba when he called for economic independence across Africa from Congo. Despite authoritative and anti-Africa western policies, there is still hope for the continent of 1.3 billion voices, unlimited natural resources, and the world's youngest youth demographic.

The Africa Continental Free Trade Area (AfCFTA) and the Digital Currency Agenda for Cross Border Trade, as defined by H.E. Mr. Wamkele Mene, the AfCFTA Secretariat secretary general, in his first press interview this year after the AfCFTA free market was launched in January 2021, highlights Africa's new, young leadership and their grasp of what it will take to free Africa both politically and economically. The roles of digital payments, digital currencies, digital tax, and/or marketplaces are clear. For example, in my first book, *The Last Digital Frontier*, I share how Jumia's recent public company listing on the New York Stock Exchange as Africa's first success (despite being German incorporated and thus not African by most measures) makes it clear to both local and foreign investors hungry for the next successful exit Africa is ready. *The Next Africa* by Jake Bright and Aubrey Hruby predicts a future in which Americans increasingly own more and more African stocks in their portfolios. This Next Africa, or what I coined "DreamAfrica," reality is being powered by solar energy, a talented and innovative youth, and activist-driven leadership like H.E. Paul Kagame of Rwanda. President Kagame has shown African countries, no matter their size and history, can achieve the African Union Agenda 2063 vision of "an integrated, prosperous, and peaceful Africa driven by its own citizens and representing a dynamic force in the global arena" when they believe in themselves, their people, talent, and resources, as stated on the AU website. Rather than dancing to the western tune of aid, democracy, and poverty porn at the expense of critical areas like security, decolonized education, energy independence, and sustainable health, Kagame challenges us all to create financial and innovation independence backed by the rule of local laws, not the traditionally anti-Africa western laws.

The closest we have come globally to having this adult conversation on locally driven ownership is when the European Union (EU) passed the General Data Protection Regulation (GDPR) to reign in tech firm's mass collection and commercialization of individual user data, including sensitive data like date of birth, banking information, and browsing activity or history, especially false news reports or stories on citizens. The United States of America (USA), as usual, is pursuing an "innovation first, legislation later" approach contrary to its more conservative cousin, the EU. So, it came as no surprise when US firms were given five years' headway, as reported by NBC, to prepare and implement GDPR compliance, they fell short. US firms to this date are still rushing to interpret, let alone understand, the implications, both legal and financial, of the EU GDPR. Google and Facebook have both seen their fair share of criticism and fines from the EU GDPR enforcement agencies to counter the US firm's violation of European citizens' data. In Europe, the user or individual has certain ownership of digital data, including the right to be forgotten (request removal of defamatory content or sensitive data like arrest records). It is the exact opposite in the US, where corporations often have exclusive and perpetual rights to Internet activity and user data, as has been the case with Internet traffic data owned by broadband companies like Comcast and Verizon.

One such controversial law in the EU GDPR is the "right to be forgotten" clause that allows EU citizens the right to ask Internet companies to delete information about them from their websites and/or digital ecosystems. Google has found itself at the end of this law, having paid over one hundred thousand euros in fines to settle and often comply with requests to "be forgotten" by EU citizens and billions in US dollars for advertising to children, according to NBC. Technical challenges here include the search, mapping, and deletion of data related to such complaints, but also the gap that may create in existing data, analysis, and related Internet activity. The EU Commission has crafted the ultimate weapon for US firms and global firms being liable to up to twenty million euros or 4 percent of the **company's** annual turnover, whichever is higher for violation of GDPR as stated by the EU Commission website. Thus, the EU has kept its citizens' data protected while keeping US and global tech firms in check as they seek global expansion and domination at the expense of individual privacy and agency online as analyzed by the Electronic Privacy Information Center (EPIC) website. As of May 2021, the EU data privacy watchdog denied Facebook's request to extend EU US data transfer protocols. The court ruled Facebook must separate EU, Ireland, and US data and end all data transfer programs, a move that will have lasting impacts on cloud and digital operations for multinationals globally, according to the Associated Press.

The US, not to be left out, still lacks a comprehensive federal policy for data privacy but has specific mandates being implemented from state to state to complement existing sensitive data protection laws, such as the US Children's Online Privacy Protection Act (COPPA) and California Data Breach Law. Since their passage, YouTube and Apple have both paid up to fines for violating COPPA and relaunched safer family-friendly apps, as reported by CNN. Apple, in particular, is in relation to student data privacy violations, including lawsuits from parents for subscription and in-app payments supporting apps targeting kids for incremental revenue, often without parental consent, according to Channel Daily News. Play stores and marketplaces or platforms are increasingly adapting to these realities and implementing measures to allow for safer children browsing alongside those thirteen and over. One such solution is a "targets children" declaration by app developers when submitting their apps to play stores to accommodate for special presentation, curation, and review, including disabling or curation of ads, ratings, and manual review by, for example, teachers for educational apps on Google's Play Store as stated in Google's family policy. In addition to making sure apps display appropriate content, developers are asked to make sure our app (including all APIs, SDKs, and ads) complies with all applicable laws and regulations relating to children, including the US Children's Online Privacy Protection Act (COPPA) and the EU General Data Protection Regulation (GDPR).

As an entrepreneur and founder of DreamGalaxy Academy, we have likewise adapted ourselves to these realities and continue to design and develop our platform with ethical data privacy methodologies in mind. For example, we recently integrated ClassLink and got the ClassLink certification for student data protection compliance where our single sign-on and login systems abstract sensitive student data during analytics access. This is in line with our long-term commitment to not share data with third parties and embracing branded media and brand placement over ads to offer a safe, family-friendly educational experience across our platform and ecosystem. Like many companies, it is easy to get tempted by advertiser dollars, but our decision to forego ads and focus on creative revenue streams was grounded on our values first innovation strategy insulated from unethical advertiser influence. At DreamGalaxy, subscriptions, usage-based billing, and branded media allow for a more sustainable business model free from ethical dilemmas such as the price of sensitive student data.

At 3:07 p.m. EST on March 20, 2021, Dr. Jose Morey shared what drives him is being a part of things bigger than himself, and in that moment, he felt a strong connection despite our Zoom call. A physician at his core, he decided to plunge into technology and now media because it is a natural extension of who he is—a healer. Referencing Ad Astra Media as inclusive innovation at scale without knowing it, he sees it as a way for him to impact and bring healing to people who will never know him, to people he will never see or physically touch as he would a physician, and be able to outlive his own human lifespan. He adds he has enjoyed being a part of these types of projects that can go through eternity.

"I think there's people who view the world in different ways, and people who have my particular mentality see obstacles as opportunities. For example, even during COVID-19, we've been growing a following through our digital online content like our web comics; we've had organizations reach out and want to create curriculum around our content in both Spanish and English."

- DR. JOSE MOREY

Ad Astra is the most ambitious project he has undertaken because of the power media can have on education and to generations upon generations he will never ever see. Just like my business partner, Franco Abott, and I with our DreamGalaxy platform, Dr. Jose is hoping he can change the entire landscape of societies over time. He knows it's not going to just be him, but he wanted to create comics and animations or docs to share with other distribution platforms interested in the US and abroad so this will essentially end up being impactful way beyond just the few people who can have Netflix or Disney+. Identity, whether in tech, education, media, or innovation, there is no doubt a critical driver for both access and representation in ethical leadership and inclusive innovation for a Cashless Society.

CHAPTER 6

OWNERSHIP IN A CASHLESS SOCIETY

―

"Only a drunkard would accept these terms."
- TANZANIA PRESIDENT JOHN MAGUFULI CANCELING A CHINESE LOAN WORTH TEN BILLION DOLLARS SIGNED BY HIS PREDECESSOR, JAKAYA KIKWETE, TO CONSTRUCT A PORT AT MBEGANI CREEK IN BAGAMOYO WITH A THIRTY-YEAR LOAN GUARANTEE AND NINETY-NINE-YEAR UNINTERRUPTED LEASE.

What is happening across Africa in decolonizing innovation and trade as well as finance is an extension of the efforts in India. The Indian government, inspired by its influential export, human capital, technology, and leadership talent like Alphabet Inc. CEO Pichai Sundararajan, a.k.a. "Sundar Pichai," who also runs Google, its subsidiary, has boasted support for local innovations both through policy and financial backing. Indians are equally responding to the challenge by extending China's strategy of supporting local innovations against foreign or imported technologies in key strategic areas, a trend piloted by the US and now mastered by emerging markets who also often hold critical inputs from talent to minerals. For example, India sees Amazon and Google as threats to local innovations. According to TechCrunch, India has implemented protective measures such as a 2 percent digital tax and a prohibition on foreign firms like Amazon or their affiliates selling directly to Indian consumers. This is a move to support India e-commerce, payments, and automation ventures, as analyzed in a *NY Times* article on decolonizing tech. With this political and local population support, Indian firms like their Chinese counterparts are thriving and increasing in valuation while US ventures limited by the ever-shrinking US market are forced to partner with or acquire these locally grown solutions to achieve the necessary scale and relevance.

A deeper look at India's resistance to foreign innovations can be seen through the analogy of the initial Japanese resistance to the gun. Like modern India resisting foreign technology transfer without localization, the Japanese, fully trustful of their culture and samurai heritage, resisted mass adoption of firearms at a time when they were being pushed by the West across the world's territories. The Japanese for decades continued to successfully defend themselves with the sword in true testament to the influence trust and culture have on mass adoption of innovations. In India, for example, before selling stakes worth over twenty billion dollars in Jio Platforms and more than six billion dollars in Reliance Retail to marquee foreign investors as reported by TechCrunch, Ambani famously made a speech in 2019 in which he urged the need to protect Indians' data in patriotic terms. "We have to collectively launch a new movement against data colonization. For India to succeed in this data-driven revolution, we will have to migrate the control and ownership of Indian data back to India—in other words, Indian wealth back to every Indian," he said to TechCrunch.

There is an underlying lesson here I personally realized during my junior year undergraduate policy class: culture and local relevance are important, if not the most important, parts of mass adoption and sustainability for technologies and innovations. As we say at DreamGalaxy, "Trust culture." DreamGalaxy, through its innovation studio and advisory model, now trains, advises, and funds ethical innovators to launch, grow, and scale inclusive innovations across education, FinTech, and health tech, among other critical sectors. We do this by focusing on Africa-based and Africa-focused ventures, as well as partnering with global accelerators and investment funds to deliver data-driven expertise and African strategy that includes cultural, social, and economic localization of the ideas, teams, and deployment of capital.

The Indian government under Narendra Modi in 2020–2021 has seized on this mandate to commit to a large biometric data and digital identity project for millions of Indians, both rural and urban, as well as integrating and supporting open-connected and scalable service delivery through mobile and digital IDs, payments, and of course, automation (Ai). Despite initial western criticism and lack of confidence, India is on track to deliver an inclusive Cashless Society with digital service delivery at the core. Of course, technology is a means to an end and not an end in itself. However, the increasing trend of big, bold government support both politically and economically for local and youth or women-driven innovation across the emerging markets is a signal to a new era of innovation. In this era, the technologies we design must reflect us and the diverse, complex, and beautiful world we live in across cultures and borders. The white male in Silicon Valley, Texas, or New York may, after all, no longer have all the keys to the digitized Cashless Society, and that is a great thing for all mankind.

No other sector has pushed this idea of local ownership and innovation other than the FinTech or digital banking sector in India. The Indian FinTech success is now inspiring other sectors to form similar communities and networks tasked with developing local innovations in critical areas like web or mobile browsing, e-commerce, health, transport, Ai, and yes, even education. With its large population and Google's recent support for Hindi and other Indian languages in addition to English, there is now seamless integration of localization and near real-time translations across sites, apps, and services. In India, and soon globally, one no longer has to know English or any other foreign language to effectively be included in the Cashless Society. From grandparents to mothers and children, India is onboarding its society to the digital network backed by biometric security, automated data, service, and communication delivery. In a world where living off-grid often means a lack of banking, health, education, and other critical services, the Indian government is modeling how service delivery can be inclusive and accessible by design, not as an afterthought.

Billions of unbanked globally and millions of underserved communities are no longer the exception, but the norm is thanks to ethical leadership and inclusive innovators from all corners of the world adapting existing technologies to their own local needs and reality, rather than importing through a technology transfer mindset of the West. Google has adapted quickly, thanks to their Indian-born CEO, by localizing all their services, e.g., supporting Hindi and other regional languages natively as well as partnering with Indian payments companies for their Google Pay service, according to *India Today*. What works in Kansas does not necessarily work in Kolkata, so most US firms are shocked to learn decades or years into their innovation, "We are not in Kansas anymore," an expression I borrow from the 1939 US movie, *The Wizard of Oz*. In the movie, Dorothy says to her dog at one point, "Toto, I've a feeling **we're not in Kansas anymore**," a phrase that has come to mean **we** have stepped outside of what is considered normal and entered a place or circumstance that is unfamiliar and uncomfortable.

This fear of the unknown is nothing new to humanity, specifically the "White Man," since colonial times when forced assimilation was the norm. In a much-needed reversal of fate, the new global majority, from Africa to China and India and across the world, is unlocking the world's real potential traditionally hidden by neocolonial and neoliberal policies that seek to profit from the status quo. Institutionally, through geopolitics, monetary policy, and trade, the status quo, backed by the West, is crumbling. Emerging markets, inspired by China and India, are waking up to their own reality instead of the West's illusionary dream. Emerging market-inclusive innovators are creating solutions that are not only culturally responsive but also accessible to all across cultures and borders.

China, once the sleeping dragon, is awake and no stranger to long-term strategic planning, having survived the difficult cultural revolution era. **Xi Jinping**, the chairman of China's Communist Party (CCP), is no stranger to strategy and has already left his mark by consolidating power. Xi is also reeling in the party to back his agenda to realize his One-China policy vis-à-vis Hong Kong and/or Taiwan as well as accelerate the Belt and Road Initiative in addition to other strategic industry targets. His strategy's success can be measured by Chinese progress such as increased trademarks and patent registrations, military equipment manufacturing, and semiconductor or chip manufacturing prioritization as reported by the Council on Foreign Relations (CFR) and the Brookings Institute. China is leveraging both hard and soft power globally to win and hold on to allies both old and new. With its growing military and economic prowess, a nuclear power herself and a permanent member of the UN Security council, China is in a comfortable position of number two as a superpower after the US. China's awareness of the global responsibilities and ethical attention that comes from being number one seems to delay it claiming the first position, despite perhaps being there already. Instead, China has decided to play the long game with the US and any other emerging adversaries, as highlighted by its growing presence in the South China Sea reported by the BBC.

This arrival of China was, in 2020, complemented by the Chinese consolidation of power in Hong Kong by establishing and enforcing the Chinese "Patriot Act" that would favor pro-mainland China politicians and leaders in elections, make it easier to extradite Hong Kong residents to mainland China for trial, and create a new China security office to oversee this new unification mandate, according to *Fortune*. Where China's hard power mirrors Russia's Vladimir Putin's strong pro-Russia vision and USSR reunification ideal, China's soft power, likewise, mirrors the US/EU global allyship agenda. China, over the last decade, has rolled out billions of dollars in infrastructure capital both as loans and human capital to build and connect the world through its Belt and Road Initiative of roads, rails, and ports, dubbed the Silk Road of the twenty-first century.

Similarly, "The African Union Agenda 2063: The Africa We Want" seeks to secure a self-sufficient home to 1.3 billion people and the world's youngest population with over 50 percent under the age of thirty years, as well as one of the world's largest digital/mobile money userbase via Safaricom's M-PESA and other telecoms like Airtel, as per African Union reports. African countries, both individually and through the African Union, have, despite US and EU caution, largely received and warmed up to China's capital, infrastructure, and human capital strategy such as military training and/or port construction. Though largely a success from a China allyship perspective, China has modified the loan terms and continues to adapt to the increasing resistance and decolonization efforts of African leaders, as well as the global diaspora. The late Tanzanian president, Magufuli, for example, rejected a one-hundred-year port development and operations plan by China that would have charged Tanzanians' hefty fees for using their own port even after its construction was funded by Chinese debt and built by only Chinese labor as captured by *International Business Times*. They say when it comes to agreements and deals, the devil is in the details. China, despite its initial colonial and extraction-based development model, is adapting faster than the US and EU to meet African demands as part of Xi's diplomacy and trade through mutual respect philosophy. It is critical to understand with the youngest youth demographic and high unemployment across Africa, African governments do not have the luxury to prioritize only foreign workers, contractors, or experts over local talent in need of both meaningful work as well as lifelong experience to build the Africa they want. Thus, the colonial World Bank and IFC mindset of bundling funding with unethical asset grabbing (from land to banks and monopolistic market share in the case of French companies) needs to stop for Africa and emerging markets to ideate, create, own, and realize their own Cashless Society.

The "China is colonizing Africa" narrative is mainly fueled by the West, like the US former secretary of state, Mike Pompeo, and the EU, which see their extraction-based policies in Africa under threat. The US/EU skepticism echoes some valid concerns by Africans on the continent and around the world. This US/EU criticism, however, is meaningless, as it lacks the authenticity of non-hypocrisy. The US and EU only care to the extent their decades of free and/or cheap access to emerging market minerals and resources, including human capital via brain drain, are under threat. Rather than counter with more humane and ethical solutions, the US and EU are resorting to their familiar playbook of propaganda and manipulation followed by threats of military force and/or "sponsored coups" to install more complicit governments, as recently seen in Libya, South Sudan, and South Africa, among other puppet regimes.

There is an increase in EU and US funding as foreign direct investment (FDI) toward Africa over the last decade. However, the racist statements by both the United Kingdom's (pre-Brexit) prime minister, Boris Johnson, and then-US president, Donald J. Trump, toward Africa and Africans in general are a clear indication of the level of white supremacist ideology that drives global policy from the self-declared police of the world. With such a lack of moral and ethical leadership, it is high time the US acknowledges there is a lot of learning from others, healing of the historically excluded, and liberation of the oppressed needed to be done. This could be within the US via reparations, actual equal justice under the law, equal pay, etc., and abroad via supporting locally driven leadership, like in Rwanda. The US could also reduce technology transfer by supporting local innovation, like endorsing mobile banking and remittance service M-PESA in Kenya instead of technology transfer only, to deliver a Cashless Society for all.

China, Russia, and India are increasingly aware of this void in global ethical leadership and commitment and exploiting it to align the world with their own political agendas. The US is still revered globally, but not in the same light it was during and soon after the second World War. For the last two decades (2000–2020), the US, despite having had its first Black president, Barack Hussein Obama, and first female vice president, Kamala Harris, has highlighted the dilemma of the American dream and idealism: that all (wo)men (regardless of sex, as per Supreme Court interpretation) are created equal. By trying—but continually failing—to live up to this ideal, as evidenced by the 2020 #DefundThePolice anti-police brutality demonstrations and campaigns highlighting unequal access to justice under the law in the US, the world is more aware despite US-positive image narrative and propaganda of the limitations and challenges in implementing its own ideals at home, let alone preaching or enforcing them abroad. This is ultimately emboldening young people and ethical leaders in their countries to take more ownership of their future by innovating locally and aspiring to scale or partner globally, including with the ever-ready US. The push, as led by China, India, Russia, and some countries across Africa, such as Rwanda, is for mutual respect and equal opportunity or partnerships. The US is unfortunately not used to nor ready to answer the request for trade and investment based on mutual respect, as it contradicts its historic preach and bully tactic, i.e., American exceptionalism that experts, including US treasury secretary Janet Yellen, warn against.

They say charity begins at home, and in Africa, and perhaps most of the world, one cannot succeed in the world when there is unresolved conflict at home. While the global drug and terrorism wars have served as a perfect distraction from America's original sin and lifelong challenge— racism, slavery, or addiction to free and low wage labor—there is less room for such "un-American" values in the Cashless Society of the twenty-first century and beyond. Unlike Hollywood movies as countered by Nollywood from Nigeria, Chinese films, and Bollywood from India, among other emerging narrative industries, the future is diverse, inclusive, and ethical. The American ideals are, after all, human ideals, and it is time America embraced that reality rather than pushing America as the exception. By pushing American ideals as human ideals and living by those, America may yet have a chance to influence, lead, and/or contribute to the broader geopolitical direction of emerging technologies in a Cashless Society. Otherwise, the decentralized revolution will impact the next generation of innovations and designs in resistance to a hypocritical and often militarized agenda that does not meet the truth and fact test of home.

Not all is gloom and doom in the land of the free and home of the brave, the USA. On April 5, 2021, *The Wall Street Journal* reported a Supreme Court decision on Oracle vs. Google with a news headline that read, "Google Wins Multibillion Dollar Copyright Fight with Oracle in Supreme Court," adding a lower court had ruled Google's Android operating system infringed Java copyrights held by Oracle. The Supreme Court ruled for Alphabet Inc.'s Google in a multibillion-dollar battle with Oracle Corporation over elements of Google's Android smartphone-operating system. *The Wall Street Journal* added this decision could weaken software copyright protections but allow developers more room to build on each other's products, concluding in Justice Stephen Breyer's words, "Google's copying did not violate the copyright law." For developers, tech innovators, and even governments, this opens Pandora's box for the historically US-dominated tech field to be open to "fair use" copying and innovation by other regions from China to India to Africa across industries without the market barrier of fear of copyright infringement litigation or trolling. Ownership, it is clear, across its various definitions and manifestations from state in China to individual in the US and patents or copyright for corporations and innovators, holds the key to the digitized and automated Cashless Society of our time.

Dr. Jose Morey's experience at NASA, Hyperloop, and other space-related projects led him to the show planet space initiative and working on a lot of outreach things with Univision. When I interviewed him, he shared how he worked with

NASA doing outreach for Hispanic communities talking and inspiring them to go into the fields of space. Through the Space Foundation, he has been a judge for the Space Technology Hall of Fame and also furthers teacher initiatives promoting more STEM through space-based media for teachers. Here, students and adults alike are introduced to STEM and AI perspectives through his edutainment company, Ad Astra Media. He adds exclusive education and innovation leave the underrepresented with low-paying jobs that are increasingly being automated away. For technology to be equitable, such demographics deserve digital skills and upskilling programs to prepare them for the Cashless Society that is mostly digital and automated. Dr. Morey clarifies inclusive access does not have to be free but, rather, through hybrid models that make ecosystems sustainable. He argues in a free ecosystem, the user is the product as their data is commercialized, as is the case for most social media like Facebook and Instagram and perhaps metaverses in the future.

CHAPTER 7

TRUST IN A CASHLESS SOCIETY

"Boeing is committed to restore trust, and we'll do it one airplane at a time."
- BOEING SAID TO THE BBC.

No American story illustrates the challenges of automation, data-driven manufacturing, and dynamic operations more than Boeing, the largest global aerospace manufacturer and US exporter. Boeing executives, according to recently released memos and investigation reports from their plane crashes shared with BBC, knew of the software defects yet often launch and continue selling their planes—in particular, model 737 MAX—instead of recalling them for repairs. It is clear the error here is human and due to a lack of ethical leadership from both management and the board of directors. Software glitches are a norm but are usually addressed or should be taken seriously, especially in critical operations and devices like transportation—think Tesla self-driving cars. Boeing knew of these deficiencies for over a decade yet chased cash via airline sales, according to a lengthy BBC exposé. Like a hungry viper striking to kill, Boeing allegedly continued faulty flight operations at the expense of thousands of lives over multiple crashes, including the Ethiopian Airlines Flight ET302 and Lion Air Flight 610 accidents, asserts BBC. The underlying issue is as a humanity, we are trained to comply, not question, and as such, bottom line or profit maximization, not a sustainable or ethical welfare of a society, is the rewarded, reinforced goal from parenting to education and work.

Boeing, in a truly American way of doing business, initially deflected any and all accountability, instead, setting up its own investigative team. The internal Boeing team was tasked with proving this was a mechanical issue, not software deficiency, which would have made the airline(s), not Boeing, liable. The Ethiopian government was smart enough to conclude its own investigation of the black box before handing it over to foreign investigators, as the truth would have been lost or swept under the rug. Thanks to their ethical leadership in Ethiopia, Boeing has been forced to review all their operations and to suspend all flights with the models impacted as far as 2020 was recommended by the US Federal Aviation Authority (FAA) until updates were made.

The loss of life was shamelessly not enough to stop Boeing from continuing operations and sales, and the board is still recovering from this damage. According to BBC, Boeing's now-former chief executive, Dennis Muilenburg, initially brushed off calls for resignation. BBC adds he soon left within weeks and was visibly uncomfortable as he faced unremitting harsh questioning while sitting yards away from relatives of those lost aboard ET302. He admitted Boeing had "made some mistakes" on his watch and "discovered some things we didn't get right," according to

BBC and NPR. Some argue the recent board changes are not enough to guarantee a change in a risky company culture that puts human life at risk every day airlines are released without the right compliance and safety standards. But in business, one's loss is another's gain, as Airbus, the second-largest seller of large airplanes, has been quick to fulfill this unmet demand as well as position itself as a safer airline brand that takes compliance and safety seriously, according to *The New York Times*. Other Chinese airlines have also seen an opening and filled in local market sales in Asia, especially China.

Boeing's recovery, though rushed by management and the board, is far from over, given they seem to be prioritizing cash over human safety and are afraid to keep losing market share and brand relevance, as investigated by *The Verge*. For Boeing to fully recover, they must go above and beyond the traditional American corporation apology and actually make meaningful institutional changes in both management and the board. Boeing might as well provide personalized compensation funds and programs for the families of those who lost their loved ones through what was, to many, clearly Boeing's negligence. The ever-present ethical dilemma of doing the right thing should be balanced with shareholder responsibility as an unethical board and management can surely not be a good value for shareholders in the long run anyway. Contrary to the myth that corporations are too powerful and, thus, individuals are helpless, individuals actually do hold power, as most software is based on user metrics and actions. The problem is we fundamentally believe we are powerless until we act and others join us, as we will explore in Chapter Nine through Eleven. Today's companies actually react to social or user pressure, as do the courts, as seen by the Boeing-App Store wars (Epic vs. Google and Epic vs. Apple), Facebook misinformation, and the Robinhood #MemeTocks scandal.

BBC reported, in 2018, a senior manager on the production line, Ed Pierson, emailed the head of the 737 Program to warn the rush to produce new aircraft was causing serious problems. "I know how dangerous even the smallest of defects can be to the safety of an airplane. Frankly, right now, all my internal warning bells are going off. For the first time in my life, I'm sorry to say I'm hesitant about putting my family on a Boeing airplane," he said in an email sent on June 9, 2018—nearly five months before Lion Air Flight 610 plunged into the Java Sea. The lesson with Boeing is technology is not the problem, but rather the lack of ethics and values from the people designing, approving, and/or regulating said technology.

BBC adds doubt persists, and in its final report, the US House Transportation and Infrastructure Committee stated the current regulatory system is broken:

> *"...Producing a compliant aircraft that proved unsafe should have been an immediate wakeup call to both Boeing and the FAA. The current regulatory system...is broken...Unfortunately, serious questions remain as to whether Boeing and the FAA have fully and correctly learned the lessons behind the MAX failures."*
>
> - US HOUSE TRANSPORTATION AND INFRASTRUCTURE COMMITTEE AS TOLD TO BBC.

The Wall Street Journal reported Boeing will end up paying seventeen million dollars in fines, the maximum federal mandate, and an additional ten million dollars is the recommended improvements for compliance and quality assurance.

Despite the COVID-19 pandemic and other strange realities, 2020 was the year for political commentary, racial tension, and yes, digital expertise. As if we were actors commissioned for one large, intergalactic stage performance, all mere mortals were forced to halt their goals, dreams, plans, and lives to survive, care for each other, and yes, even reflect and reckon with history. For some, it was a welcome opportunity to finish real estate development projects that had been put on hold. For others, it was the straw that broke the camel's back, while for others, it was an outright violation of their "God-given freedom and right" to be privileged and oppress others. Regardless of where one found oneself on the spectrum—and a wide spectrum it was given the increased racial, economic, and political divide globally and especially in the US—the gods, aliens, or spirits depending on one's religious belief must have been entertained by each of our reactions. For those seeking a comic reexamination of this global performance for the artificial intelligence observing us from other galaxies, please rewatch *Long Live 2020*, a comic documentary that uses original footage and comic actors to archive our performance for eternity.

So, yes, 2020 is the year Twitter banned US President Trump, the US Congress grilled Big Tech CEOs as reported by France 24, and Capitol riots or the plot to reverse voting rights in a Cashless Society all happened within weeks or months of each other. The CEOs included Jack Dorsey from Twitter, Mark

Zuckerberg from Facebook, Satya Nadella from Microsoft, and Pichai Sundararajan, better known as Sundar Pichai, from Google. America, in Malcolm X's words, seemed to be reaping the seeds it had sowed since the origins of the country. Rome, Caesar, and the Republic were on the line, and by God's grace—or shall we say, by the sanity of individual will and agency called democracy—was it saved before it was too late. Despite wishes for a merry Christmas and a positive start of the year in 2021, the election results denial due to mail-in voting and electronic vote counting in some areas, Capitol riots and unending police brutality continued a 2020 #ThisIsAmerica trend. Even Big Tech continued to be in the spotlight, as evidenced by the #GameStop saga where Robinhood, a self-proclaimed pro-mass trading app for the people, decisively cut off automated trading order flow from Reddit's #WallStreetBets trading community, as reported by CNBC. According to Yahoo!, Jaime Rogozinski, who *founded* the *subreddit* in 2012, says he did it looking for a more active way to trade investment ideas within a community. These #MemeStock traders bought GameStop stock in resistance to elite Wall Street fund managers shorting the stock, i.e., betting against the company in hopes the stock would decline. Coincidentally, these elites included Citadel LLC, a majority stake owner in Robinhood, which Robinhood seemed to pick over the masses when it stopped the order flow.

Millennials, locked inside with the world in chaos, turned to gaming and trading only to realize Wall Street would not go down without a fight. The decision to stop order flow from the masses is a typical Wall Street reaction ironically from Robinhood, the brand sworn to fight for the little guy, according to Bloomberg. At the core is the paid order flow model Wall Street has embraced, enabling rewards for traders or aggregators routing orders to exchanges. For Robinhood, its dilemma was routing increasing orders without the cash deposits necessary to meet the collateral/margin call obligations, according to Robinhood CEO Vladimir Tenev, seen on Bloomberg TV and interviewed by Bloomberg host Emily Chang.

According to Bloomberg, the company faces multiple legal and regulatory challenges, including a complaint from Massachusetts securities regulator alleging the app uses "aggressive" tactics to entice young, inexperienced investors while failing to protect them from taking undue risks, which Tenev refutes.

> *"The facts will come out, and it will bear out Robinhood is a customer-focused company operating with the highest standards of integrity."*
>
> - TENEV ON BLOOMBERG TV.

Robinhood chose to protect elite Wall Street investors over fulfilling its duty to its investors, the mass traders. Either way, as the Securities and Exchange Commission (SEC) and US Congress investigation into the #GameStop saga, or shall we say Wall Street vs. Reddit Traders, shows the house always wins. A lesson we hope mass traders are learning is Wall Street mirrors Las Vegas when it comes to bets and winning.

Financial wins and losses in the US seem to follow political winds despite progress since the Civil Rights Act of 1964, which was to reduce voter suppression efforts. Pro- and post-Jim Crow voter suppression efforts included guessing the number of jelly beans in a jar or presenting state identification and other reading quizzes before being allowed to vote, which was meant to hinder a historically enslaved and excluded African American population. For context, slaves were not allowed to learn to read, and as such, there were generational gaps in literacy even post-slavery. Thus, despite the US allowing voting rights for women among other progressive agendas like the LGBTQ rights, most Republicans embraced false information from the very top, according to NPR. The "stolen elections" and "find me the votes" propaganda by President Trump and his legal team who have since been disbarred or fined by the courts and referred to state bar associations for disbarment despite loss after loss from state to regional circuits and ultimately the Supreme Court, as reported by NBC News.

The 2020 US election and the Republican backlash to introduce a "New Jim Crow" of voter intimidation, voter suppression, and exclusion of voting rights to certain Americans of color, particularly African Americans, is an indication of the innate fear or *myth* only whites can be trusted with technology or leadership in a Cashless Society, let alone the simplest technologies like mail-in voting, QR code scanning, or digital counting. Such measures now include more punishments for election observers or clerks for minor mistakes, less use of technology—e.g., mail-in ballots—and reduced voting time, including understaffing of historically and majority "non-white" neighborhoods. From this experience alone—the fundamental right to vote in a democracy—to some, it only seems to matter if one is white and/or Republican. Such is the relevance and role of trust in a digitized Cashless Society.

Stacey Abrams has emerged as the single bravest soul in America, working to save US democracy and, ultimately, America's very foundation. From her grassroots voter registration campaigns in Georgia, having lost the governor race a few years back due to voter suppression tactics by the state, she is on a mission to make democracy accessible to all. According to the *Atlanta* magazine, "Since 1972—nearly fifty years ago—Georgia has only gone blue three times: in 1976 and 1980, the state voted for our own Jimmy Carter, and in 1992, Georgia picked Bill Clinton for the presidency. Otherwise, it has been a steady red vote." And luck is on her side as she flipped Georgia blue for the first time since 1992, according to Nate Silver's FiveThirtyEight website during the 2020 election, allowing Democrats to retain a majority in both the House and Senate. The New Jim Crow is making its way across America, state by state, county by county, but one can only hope Americans and their executive, legislative, and judicial systems will embrace the fundamental values and beliefs "all (wo)men are created equal" and reject the "New Jim Crow" agenda and propaganda. This increasing lack of trust across political, racial, and class lines has long-term implications in the technologies designed, implemented, and used by communities at home in the US as well as abroad, from civic engagement to education and healthcare access, among other society needs, including free enterprise.

"America never was America to me," writes American poet and author James Baldwin of the ethical dilemmas surrounding the African Americans in America who are often sold one dream only to live another (a recurring unequal justice under the law nightmare). It is clear technology, a practical solution in the twenty-first century, is not the problem but, rather, a lack of ethical or moral foundation. This is ironically more extreme in the party of Christian and family values that fail to bring to reality the core principle in the US constitution, that "all…are created equal." Tech activists and innovators have a role to play in saving practical, accessible, and not exclusionary democracy by increasing reliable information access, voter registration nudges, and protecting elections from both foreign and these days' local influence. Needless to say, the influence of cash on US elections plays a role here, and in an ethical Cashless Society, income disparities and/or corporate or lobbyist contributions should not determine the fate of communities and citizens but rather their vote, aspirations, and civic engagement.

This influence of money in the US is not new, as there is a long history of financial institutions excluding people of color through redlining zip codes and other practices to leave out generations from economic growth via credit and/or real estate denial. JPMorgan Chase, Wells Fargo, US Bancorp, and others recently announced they will factor in information from applicants' checking or savings accounts at other financial institutions to increase their chances of being approved for credit cards starting late 2021. *The Wall Street Journal* reports the effort, if successful, would mark a significant change in the underwriting tactics of big banks, which for decades have enshrined credit scores and credit reports as the main tools to determine who gets a loan. They generally reflect a person's borrowing history in the US, including whether they pay their loans on time. *The Wall Street Journal* adds what most ought to already know, that those who pay only with cash or debit cards, or who are new to the US, often don't have credit scores. The same is true for those who have just turned eighteen. In the US, getting a credit card is a dilemma, as one needs to have a history or credit to get one, so credit approval becomes extremely difficult. Even worse, one's credit score often goes down or decreases if one pays off a debt. The credit card system, as is currently deigned as "bullshit" by one American I spoke to, is exclusionary and really unreliable (hard to navigate for both lenders and borrowers).

Thus, from Boeing, to mail-in ballots, to ballot-counting machines, to banking, to particular credit scores in a Cashless Society, there seems to be a gap in what is considered approved and legal behavior vs. what ought to be the ethical and inclusive way of doing things. America, like the rest of the world, has a lot of ethical reckoning to do. American business board of directors have an ethical responsibility to society to not only save lives but also only approve ethical and inclusive innovation within their organizations for their employee morale and trust, investor transparency, and increased shareholder value. The future is ethical, and values like "identity, ownership, trust, and scale" (what I call the four IoTs in my first book) are driving shareholder value through the conscious consumer revolution. Boeing's mismanagement of innovation and crisis that led to the loss of lives is a cautionary tale for all corporations, executives, and their regulators to not fail the public's trust. After all, even the invisible hand of supply and demand seems to already be influenced by these four core values of identity, ownership, trust, and scale.

Asked about the fear of or lack of trust for automation, Dr. Jose Morey, NASA, Hyperloop, and White House advisor, shared this with me during our interview in spring 2021:

"It's more raw than that; it's more brainstem early evolutionary response than automation. It goes back to just a fear of change. I think fear of change is good, healthy, and a very normal response to evolutionary disruption as you get worried. After you've been able to survive in a society or with a particular evolutionary advantage when something changes, then you're worried either you or your progeny won't be able to survive. That will always be with us because that is something that's been advantageous, at least to biological evolution. Now, if we ever evolved into some sort of combination of biologic and mechanical or biomechatronic that might be a little bit different. Then we'll be able to direct our evolution and we are very close to directing our evolution already via a lot of gene editing and silicon-based augmentation. So, we've already taken that leap to not have to worry about change as much because we direct our own evolution to a certain degree."

- DR. JOSE MOREY

Indeed, agency, peer-to-peer convenience, derivative products backed by insurance, or security depending on use case are what it may take to earn and restore trust in a Cashless Society. The final three chapters address some of this in detail, but at the core, culture and society expectations do play a role. For example, an individualistic society like America may actually be served best by peer-to-peer networks and decentralized digital ecosystems due to their "anti-government overreach mentality." Ironically, it is democratic governments that can and should be trusted to the extent they are answerable to the people. Social or communal societies like China and most of Africa, while already benefiting from decentralized finance and mobile money, could use some ethical leadership from government to aid their ecosystem credibility when it comes to international transactions. Therefore, just as Jesus stated, "Give unto Caesar what is Caesar's." Government will always have a role to play, especially via policy or legal enforcement and economic incentives. However, decentralized autonomous organizations (DAOs), as explored later, are also possible for some use cases like private enterprises and/or communal or peer-to-peer systems where the rules of engagement are voted on by the community or platform owners via a tokenized and digitized infrastructure. In a way, the individual can become and is a part of the Cashless Society through identity (digital and cultural) representation, ownership (equity and economic) through tokenization, trust through active or delegated participation, and scale through inclusive access across cultures and borders.

CHAPTER 8

SCALE IN A CASHLESS SOCIETY

—

"Apple offers a paradox of choice."
- MARQUES BOWMAN, YOUTUBE TECH VLOGGER @MKBWN

Contrary to the Western view of Africa as most of their emerging markets being poor and devoid of innovation worth supporting, China is leading the world by delivering incredible success stories. China's success stories range from Alibaba, the world's biggest IPO in the last decade on the New York Stock Exchange (NYSE), to the recent e-commerce success of SoftBank Capital-backed South Korean e-commerce firm Coupang (NYSE: CPNG) also on Wall Street's NYSE, according to *Nikkei Asia*. Southeast Asia, India, and most of Africa are all booming with new category kings in FinTech, HealthTech, education, and yes, even AI, including self-driving cars. This realization and actualization of innovation across borders and boundaries, despite decades of colonial extraction, systemic trade, and political sabotage, is evidence of what the future of innovation looks like. The global finance policies are still colonial in nature in that more trust is given to Western countries at the expense of African and other emerging markets. This sort of self-centered, exclusion-based "redlining" leaves an unequal playing field where African innovations are often penalized or even forced to domicile in the United States of America (USA) or Europe (EU) and the United Kingdom (UK) post-Brexit to achieve the same parity and not risk loss of ownership.

In an ideal world, the ethical Cashless Society would apply the same ownership and trust standards equally. Equal application of trust means an African, Chinese, European, or US company would all be given the same financial regulatory treatment. Unfortunately, we are still decades from this reality, as transactions to Africa are treated as a risk or liability while transactions from or to the West are not, as evidenced by the extravertive foreign subsidiaries and conglomerates. Innovation can only thrive in free markets and/or supported environments, and this biased regulation that is anti-African and anti-emerging markets creates an imbalance in innovation across regions and borders, which is unethical. How can international companies operating within Africa often, after countless political bribes, be seen and treated as financially compliant against local and innovative brands?

This moral hypocrisy is designed to offer an unfair advantage to Western companies, and, ultimately, countries must end this hypocrisy of "fair trade." Emerging markets are taking charge and owning more of their innovation stories and journeys, starting with regional banking, digital or mobile banking, and now global IP ownership and registration. The

Cashless Society will not be "Made in the West," but, rather, it shall be "Made Locally and Connected Globally" via a mesh of decentralized nodes and other microservices due to the relevance and impact of ownership in a Cashless Society. The innovator of e-commerce and mobile banking in India has as much a right to scale and grow internationally as the hacker or nerd in Silicon Valley, California. That is the true competition China, Russia, India, Brazil, and African nations aspire to. The successful examples of this model can be found in Southeast Asia, such as Indonesia and Singapore, where innovation from e-commerce to hospitality and indoor farming is challenging and changing global supply chains.

Beyond banking the unbanked, a service needed by about four billion people globally, there is an increasing need for inclusion across all areas of innovation despite the digital divide. From education to mobile money, traditional models of cash-based businesses are being disrupted across Africa and the world. The consumer is king now, and service delivery is mobile first and human always. This means localization and cultural relevance will continue to drive mass adoption and sustainability of Cashless Society innovations. For example, M-PESA's success as the world's largest and simplest mobile banking network started thriving in Kenya as local innovation and then across East Africa, according to Bloomberg. This is ideal and better than the slow and hard-to-scale traditional bank policy in West Africa that requires cash banking licenses for mobile money operators and excludes non-fiat or cash banking licensed telecoms or new local digital banking innovators in the process. The M-PESA success is due to the consumer-focused innovation mandate in Kenya that blends local languages like Swahili and the simplicity of communication like texting. M-PESA ultimately delivers meaningful, inclusive, and accessible banking, saving, and trading services to over a quarter billion people across Africa. Young people and women traditionally excluded from business and the economy are now owners of their own destinies, starting, running, and growing SMEs across Africa and soon the world. Thus, ownership refers to the IP ownership as well as the inclusive access to the developed IP by the masses for both scale and impact.

Mobile Health Kiosks and telehealth are other examples of communities taking ownership of their health and welfare rather than relying on cash-strained government or private hospitals. Entrepreneurs are launching innovative mobile clinic solutions that accept mobile money, as well as tapping into mobile electronic records management systems. For example, Karisimbi Technologies in Rwanda, which I advise and mentor, is helping digitize most of the government hospitals and soon private health networks as well. The founder, Angelo C. Igitego, told me during one of our advisory calls the goal is to expand into coupon discounts for families and hospital visitors. These digital coupons or credits and discounts could then be honored by hospitals as cobranded digital ID cards with the potential to add insurance companies or offer microinsurance services as part of the platform. This focus on data privacy and ownership, localization, and cost savings of up to 80 percent just from digitizing healthcare records management across East Africa and eventually the whole of Africa is the exact kind of ethical and inclusive innovations needed in a Cashless Society. It is inspiring to see the days of relying on unethical hospital intake practices at government hospitals that rely on understaffed paper record keeping and cash-first intake may soon be over. They will instead be complemented or replaced with digital records intake and mobile payment options. As a son of the soil, having grown up in Uganda and seen the challenges of hospital administration and healthcare delivery, this is a game changer. Not only will knowledge and information sharing between doctors and patients improve, but also the health consultations by experts on treatments, recovery support, and home-based healthcare such as both preventive health campaigns as well as chronic health management for diseases like diabetes, HIV, and/or recently COVID-19.

"Data ownership and privacy as a right" is becoming the norm across Europe due to the European General Data Protection Regulation (GDPR). Meanwhile, in America, data is by law the sole property of Internet and technology companies. The US exceptions for medical and other sensitive data use cases are often bundled in the healthcare and finance systems and not in the easy access ownership of individual users or citizens. This contrast is likely to shape future global strategies and deliberations on the best way forward. Even agreeing on what privacy, let alone ownership, means will vary from country to country as well as cultural context. As such, today's data privacy policies cannot be easily transferable or enforced across borders. Edward Snowden, a former National Security Agency (NSA) contracting analyst turned activist, showed us all this when he revealed the secret depth and normalcy of mass surveillance in the US. Today, the Internet community is more aware of what privacy means and/or the lack thereof in the US, including from the US government, and is actively pushing back via activism for policy change as well as the use of more private communications like the Signal and

Telegram apps. As such, it is not easy to blanketly criticize China for its open data-tracking practices when the exact thing is being carried out by the US, including against its allies. The US has been known to secretly surveil its allies, e.g., Germany's Angela Merkel Blackberry scandal. According to a Pew Research Center survey in the US, 36 percent of the population are for and 56 percent against listening to allies' leaders calls.

There is a common Internet meme or statement that reads, "If you are not paying for the product, you are the product." The Open Data Movement has its limitations. This is despite its global footprint as well as support across Europe and in the US under Obama or in major cities like New York City. Among these open data limitations is the lack of proper data ownership and transparency across electronic systems leading to both historical bias and data manipulation. As users have no control of data, especially sensitive data, including credit scores, among other datasets, there is a delegation of responsibility to corporations when it comes to data ownership and privacy. Such is the case of public opinion or the Facebook vs. Apple data privacy battle for users' trust that, in actuality, makes the user the product. Thus, companies, despite their intentions, commercialize the data, often without the user's consent or benefit.

For Facebook, this is through targeted advertising, while for Apple, it is through a monopolistic innovation ecosystem that excludes or limits third-party applications in favor of Apple's internal software, according to *Inc.* magazine. Thus, on Facebook, the user is the product, whose activity and data powers their targeted advertising algorithm, bringing in billions in ad dollars, especially on mobile and across its apps, including third-party sites via Facebook Pixel or tracking code. Apple, similarly, would like to hoard the user data for itself, under the disguise of honoring privacy, while launching its own advertising, payments, communications, and/or security apps that compete with and often outshine third-party apps due to the unfair advantage of exclusive access and preferential treatment to user data and/or billing.

This is why Apple is fighting Facebook in the court of public opinion. This is going on while Apple is being sued in US courts by Epic Games, the distributor of the popular game *Fortnite*, for Apple's exorbitant 30 percent App Store revenue share fees on developers' apps, yet Apple's software does not incur a similar burden or cost. *The Verge* reports on Judge John Rogers' opinion. "The evidence does suggest Apple is near the precipice of substantial market power, or monopoly power, with its considerable market share," Judge John Rogers wrote—but said the antitrust claims failed in part "because [Epic] did not focus on this topic." In fact, both these arguments are similar to the 1990s Microsoft practice of installing free Internet Explorer on all Microsoft PCs against other browsers like Firefox and Google Chrome, later ruled as an antitrust case against Microsoft. This unreliability and lack of ownership in a Cashless Society for IP, data, and even access create mistrust in Internet service use. According to CNBC, the US Supreme Court stopped short of calling Apple a monopoly but recently ordered Apple to be more flexible with its App Store listing policies to allow apps to collect payments outside of the App Store billing ecosystem, a big win for consumers and developers who can now set their own prices and payment collection processions outside of

Apple's 30 percent share monopoly. The same measure has been shared by Google Play Store.

Dr. Jose Morey, during our interview, shared that, unfortunately, there will always be job losses at the beginning of a Cashless Society adoption or evolution/upgrades, a natural way of how new types of revolutions occur. As with the coal to electricity transition, Dr. Jose argues "creative destruction" is an unfortunate consequence of progress. He cautions us to make sure technology's equitable. Equitable technology means it [technology] isn't perpetuating systemic bias, but rather inclusive access, e.g., electricity for everyone and the accessible Internet leveling the playing field. Online and mobile commerce is disrupting brick-and-mortar retail stores at scale in a world where everyone is a creative person who can be their own business by making money just from being on TikTok, YouTube, or Instagram. The gig and influencer or no ownership (sharing) economy would not have been possible at the start of the Internet but is now the norm. In fact, remote work and shared online collaboration are what made life possible during COVID-19 and are likely here to stay in some shape or form.

He adds, "I believe the Internet is creating more jobs than it's taking away…Same thing for AI and automation…If you can keep it equitable, then I believe it will ultimately be a boon to the economy that could generate income by itself."

I fundamentally believe in the concept of creative destruction and lifelong learning and would love to see more youths trained in ethical, digital, and critical analysis skills as the colonial and post-colonial clerk training system is nearing its end. The future of work is dynamic, remote, and localized, not just westernized. I in no way miss my colonial-based memorization schooling in Uganda or the single-narrative education in the US. Instead, I have grown more interested in learning post-university through on-the-job training, networking at conferences, learning by doing, and leveraging online learning platforms. I founded DreamGalaxy Academy to bring cultural relevance to online learning and media distribution, and we are already impacting and partnering with hundreds of higher education institutions across Africa and the world.

When I asked Dr. Jose if doctors should be worried about AI doctors, he cautioned against self-interested thinking.

> *"Well…if AI gets to the point where it can do all sorts of diagnostic work, that means AI is doing a lot of other things as well, and that completely changes the world where you might not even need to work…Maybe we're all creatives…Or there's so much enough to go around."*
>
> - DR. JOSE MOREY, NASA, HYPERLOOP, AND WHITE HOUSE ADVISER

Dr. Jose argues the same thing with the space industry and other things or sectors. The best way forward, it seems, is to not be selfish but, rather, embrace a shared value ecosystem model whose rewards capture societal benefits and ethical concerns, not just individual convenience and/or concerns. I personally agree with this approach, as I have already seen AI make technology accessible to millions and soon billions via automating close captioning and language translation, among other dynamics, to near real-time localizations.

The issue of scale is so worrisome even ethical AI or data experts are still figuring it out:

> *"The facial recognition start-up Clearview AI is an example of what happens when information we put out in the world for one purpose gets collected and used for another—in that case, assembling an online photo database of millions of people—none of the participants really consented to. We have little control about what happens to our personal information. Even just trying to understand what happens to our data is exhausting. I have written about digital privacy for years, and I still find it extremely complicated."*
>
> - THORIN KLOSOWSKI, AN EDITOR FOR THE NEW YORK TIMES'S PRODUCT REVIEW SITE, WIRECUTTER

Such is our dilemma—technology is evolving way too fast for us to even comprehend how it works, let alone use it correctly or ethically.

In a LinkedIn post in 2021, I commended Ernst & Young Ethical AI expert Reid on his counterargument for those who feel they have nothing to hide from data privacy or automation over reach and scale. Reid argues it is not what we share initially that is problematic but, rather, what can be inferred from the aggregate or related datasets, often from disparate sources. Thus, a cybercriminal or corporation is able to piece more details in a short time about someone's identity and sensitive data such as credit score or academic grades and make life-changing analysis and decision-making that impacts the user or the public. At issue is the lack of awareness, transparency, or even consent where algorithms like the policing datasets can determine the fate of an individual without their willing participation or awareness. This is where I ask if when machines become smarter than humans, should humans surrender free will and agency to algorithms? After all, algorithms can be programmed to address the limits of human intelligence, such as being prone to mistakes, delays, and/or emotional bias. One recent example is Facebook's failure to update its algorithm even after knowing it prioritized clickbait articles and controversial topics, a bug or feature that was good for both increased user engagement and, ultimately, ad revenue. Thus, programming itself can replicate the mistakes or emotional biases of the programmers. In Mark Zuckerberg's and most coders' words, "Code is law," after Lawrence Lessig's book by the same title.

Some find this concept of AI doctors really interesting, warranting further explorations, which we do in later chapters.

> *"There are other ethical questions worth looking at besides job loss, such as problems currently found in medicine. For example, there are mounds of data showing doctors take female patients less seriously. The same is true for non-white patients (at least in the US, I haven't looked at other countries) as well as patients who happen to be overweight or have mental healthcare issues. All of these groups are more likely to be misdiagnosed, told their symptoms are psychological when they're not, or told to lose weight when they have an actual problem that needs to be treated. Could an AI do better than a human doctor at overcoming its biases? To me, this is a fascinating question. I don't know if the answer is yes, because there's also evidence tech programmed by mostly white men tends to pick up the biases of its creators."*

- ANONYMOUS US BETA READER

These social, economic, and legal questions driven by ethical inquiry are what the next few chapters are about. At the core is the hypothesis human error or values are what drive innovation and, as such, influence technology and how we interact with it. There is also exploration for fully autonomous systems that, by design, limit human interactions or bias. As such, the human impact is at the point of creation or innovation as well as the long-term effect of such automated systems. Self-training computer algorithms are good examples where their behavior changes with more data input or time, and as such, they need a form of explainability to be trusted or even understood. The answer to all our ethical dilemmas, no matter how complex, is "it depends" on context (cultural, religious, economic, legal, historic, etc.), as we still lack shared fundamental values as a human species. So, approaching life or death decisions around health or legal sentencing with empathy, old-school human judgment, and gut instinct despite its biases is preferred, but not in others like transportation, as evidenced by zero to no accidents on smart or high-speed trains in Japan.

CHAPTER 9

THE POWER OF INDIVIDUAL AGENCY AND ACTIVISM

> *"Businesses that make money by collecting and selling detailed records of private lives were once plainly described as 'surveillance companies.' Their rebranding as 'social media' is the most successful deception since the Department of War became the Department of Defense."*
> - @SNOWDEN | EDWARD SNOWDEN (MARCH 17, 2018)

Today's companies and institutions have mastered the art of communications and propaganda and often brand themselves as the exact opposite of what they do to capture the market with minimal regulation and criticism.

In 2010, my electrical engineering professor gave me a C for writing my intellectual property class essay on the eventual triumph of open source over proprietary software. I was ten years ahead of reality perhaps, or naive. After all, I had only touched a computer or interacted with the Internet four years earlier in 2006, at age eighteen, to review the email with my flight ticket details to the US from Uganda. There is a focused and unquenchable thirst Interest-based learning brings. So, coupled with years of exclusion from the Internet, particularly the digital world, I was fully aware of the opportunity before me: the chance to not only study electricity or analog circuits but also digital circuits or electronics via my electrical and computer engineering major. Needless to say, it was not an easy program, but I had a great academic mentor who saw my early interest in business and policy and advised me to minor in economics. It is with this background and my concurrent exposure to policy studies I penned my essay arguing the Google vs. Oracle case being argued at that time in the highest courts of the land (US Supreme Court) were a waste of time and resources and countered where the industry needed to be headed. Perhaps the professor felt the foundations of capitalism, the right to own and benefit from property, was attacked. On the contrary, I saw greed and the need to abuse legal systems to stifle innovation. To me, Oracle's unrelenting pursuit of Google's Java source code use, though minor, was misguided and showed a lack of innovative spirit on Oracle's side to counter the then-upstart Google. As mentioned in earlier chapters, the US Supreme Court ultimately ruled in favor of Google's "fair use" argument against Oracle in a win for open-source and code-sharing practitioners.

In my culture, the Bakonzo tribe from Kasese, Uganda, we have a saying: "One does not need to own cattle to tell when they are sick." I, too, did not need to have been born under capitalism, nor own a company, to understand Silicon Valley investor Andreessen Horowitz's words that "software was eating the world" and that open source was the means to that end but not the end itself. It's all based on a simple innovation called "Copy and Paste," or abstract referencing, a functionality that has made the Web and entire digital ecosystem what it is today. As a programming student today, it makes no sense to demonstrate originality and proprietary code development when the very libraries you are referencing have already been coded and shared by others. Rather, the power lies in innovating on top of existing code to deliver a new, valuable code base and functionality. After all, we now have software that can write or create more software and even text and improve the functionality of such code.

In today's world, we now call this the serverless and application programming interface (API) driven world that powers the future of everything, starting with the Internet of Things (IoT), from edge processing enabled mobile devices to drones and soon house appliances. As a reality check, Google's Android powers a majority over 70 percent of the world's mobile digital ecosystem and may continue to do so if American capitalism does not stand in the way, according to Statista. Absolute and unethical capitalism could allow monopolistic ecosystems like Apple to thrive against free and open innovation platforms like Google's Android OS. Further governments could add an export tax on software innovations from the US as the US-China Internet dominance rivalry escalates, as we discuss in later chapters. This means more data generated and collected and more potential for security vulnerabilities. *The Wall Street Journal* reported about the recent ransomware attack on Colonial Pipeline in the US in May 2021 that led to the company paying millions in cryptocurrency to the hackers despite the US government's disapproval to accelerate critical gas service delivery across the US.

Tuesday, May 25, 2021, *The WSJ* headline reads, "After Colonial Pipeline Hack, US to Require Operators to Report Cyber Attacks." Here, *The WSJ* is reporting the springboard for the Transportation Security Administration's new stance is the ransomware attack as well as a sharp increase in attacks against critical assets. Thus, your health, finance, safety, and yes, even privacy become controlled by an algorithm, not your own individual agency or free will. This robotic agent model of decision-making at scale is making it even easier for individuals, institutions, and nation-states to be manipulated by smart hackers and algos that often leave no trail or are hard to detect.

So what Oracle did to Google a decade ago over software code seems to be repeating itself with Apple vs. Facebook, but this time in the public opinion court, not the judicial courts, and over data privacy, not derivative code. The issue is whether applications on Device Operating Systems like Apple's iOS on mobile have the right to access, use and share personal data of the users on that device, platform, or operating system. Forbes reports that Apple, despite false marketing in the past and untested privacy claims, has gone the length to be the Data Knight for the end user, or shall we say, self-declared privacy Czar for all users on its exclusive ecosystem playing both regulator and court on all issue data related. This privacy gambit, while strategically sound for Apple's core brand appeal, may backfire in the long term as Apple draws scrutiny over its claims and practices. "We at Apple believe privacy is a fundamental human right," Apple's CEO, Tim Cook, said in a privacy-conference keynote last year in Brussels livestreamed on YouTube.

As an Android user and fan, I am confident Apple is not as secure as it claims, but it definitely tries to secure user data at the users' loss of independence to a monopolistic ecosystem bent on disincentivizing external innovation on its platform. Apple is flexing its contract-law muscle, not its privacy muscle, and gaining a publicity win in the process, according to *The Atlantic*. Crucially, Apple didn't ban Facebook from the App Store or the iPhone platform; you can still download and use Messenger, highlighting the lack of action or hypocrisy of its pro-data privacy calls, according to *The Atlantic*.

Facebook, on the other hand, is at least pretending to be upfront on its business model. We are the product as highlighted by the Cambridge Analytica report and scandal where NPR reports Facebook paid over a 653-thousand-US-dollar fine as well as the Mueller report to Congress on the 2016 Russia misinformation campaign on Facebook, according to NPR. Our sessions, data, and engagement on the platform are what power its targeted advertising businesses generating billions of dollars across its ecosystem of apps and services from Facebook to Instagram, from WhatsApp to Oculus, among others. As users, we go through phases of self-denial, mostly pseudo-threatening to leave every time we learn of how much data we are sharing and is being monetized with third parties. Most of us, in fact, convince ourselves we have nothing to hide and, as such, are fine with such extreme data collection, mapping, and sharing in perpetuity without regard for long-term privacy, security, health, and financial implications.

Facebook is the badge of honor and symbol of free speech to the extreme among us, as highlighted in recent 2006–2020 elections across the world and especially in the US. Before and after Parler, there was and is still Facebook. Long live Mark Zuckerberg as he says, "Code is law," and the hackers' way has won our freedom. We are now but humble denizens of the Zuck Nation, where advertiser dollars and budgets determine what we see in our newsfeed, who we talk to, and most importantly, news we engage with. This ultimately shapes how we see ourselves and the world around us, and if and when we take that brief but regrettable moment from Facebook's world of apps and services.

The real debate is not between Apple vs. Facebook but rather between the disillusioned power users who claim they are fully aware of their rights and the critical few asking us to pause and reflect on the present and future we deserve and want. Are we really deciding for ourselves when what we see, read, and watch and who we talk to is curated by an algorithm whose single purpose is to increase advert conversion for the advertising spend by any means necessary, including false information spreading to increase user retention and engagement? To reflect on that is to open the Pandora's box that is data privacy rights. For example, according to *The Wall Street Journal*, US district judge Yvonne Gonzalez Rogers decided Apple did not operate an illegal monopoly, though it showed monopolistic behavior after making it clear she was thinking about how previous precedent-setting cases involving Amex and a St. Louis railroad apply to the new digital economy. Apple has since updated its App Store terms to allow developers to charge for apps or bill customers from the developer website outside the App Store.

Of the Big Tech Five—Apple, Amazon, Facebook, Google, and Microsoft—nothing screams *"caution"* than Google's cash-driven pivot from "don't do evil" as its ethical code of conduct to "be evil" in a world where US and other government contracts, personal data, and cultural appropriation are the new shiny object, according to Gizmodo. When I asked him in March 2021 what this book, *Cashless Society 101*, can be summed up as, Patrick K. Lim, legal scholar and author of *Machine See, Machine Do*, shared to him, Cashless Society means, "If money is the root of all evil, then an ethical Cashless Society should be the source of all good" (New Degree Press, December 2021). For Google, the choice at the moment seems to be "cash over ethics" despite a global COVID-19 pandemic and a world in need of a moral or ethical campus. Are we being too harsh on these well-meaning institutions? After all, I am writing this from Google Docs, a Google service, and enjoying Google Fi connectivity, and oh yes, the American dream? I say we absolutely should criticize, debate, aspire, and yes, do better. Self-improvement is but a human trait. Google can do better too. Activism, regulatory policy, and consumer demand can have an impact. More importantly, it is always time to do the right thing. We should never despair just because we feel overwhelmed or the technocrats are too big to fail. Resistance is not futile because change starts with each one of us before we can change or impact the world.

One such hero is Timnit Gebru, one of the few Black women in the ethical AI research field, who on December 23, 2020, was fired from the AI research team at Google after she published her findings critical of Google's AI even when her employee annual reviews and contributions had been hailed internally as reported by *The Washington Post*. According to

The Washington Post, Timnit pushed back against generic and vague ethical requirement terms like "make things fair" in preference for building institutional structures and documentation tools for "when people want to do the right thing." It adds she was pushing back against the "black box of algorithmic accountability inside Google-annotating the companies' claims with contradictory data, drawing connections to larger systemic issues, and illuminating the way internal AI ethics efforts can break without oversight or change in incentives to corporate practices and power structures."

Silicon Valley's self-policing by predominantly white, Asian, and male falls far from Wall Street's self-policing, as argued by Rumman Chowdhury, a former global lead for responsible AI at Accenture and now CEO at Parity. According to *The Washington Post,* "It is being framed as the AI optimists and the people really building the stuff [versus] the rest of us negative Nellies, raining on their parade." In fact, the underlying challenge for American innovation is exactly that: a lack of ethical involvement in both education and the workplace with conversations around ethics, race and/or environment, social, and governance (ESG) seen as both anti-capitalism and ultimately anti-American by the gullible masses. Questioning the American innovator or businessman is apparently the equivalent of religious sin for our time, and as such, a culture of mediocrity and unethical leadership is being tolerated and rewarded. In *The Washington Post,* he sums up the lack of ethical leadership in the all or majority (white) male executive board think Apple and boys' club mentality today (think Google) as "…it's like the boys will make the toys and then the girls will have to clean up."

Gebru's published paper highlights four categories of harm: "the environmental effect of computing power; the inscrutability of massive datasets used to train the models; the opportunity cost of the "hype" around claims these models can understand language, as opposed to identifying patterns; and the danger the real-sounding text generated by such models could be used to spread misinformation." Gebru sums up her treatment at Google as reflective of the industry in general, where women and minorities or BIPOC have no voice in a decision-making hierarchy that is often white, male, and in America. According to *The Washington Post*, she shared, "It's sad, the scientific community respects us a lot more than anybody inside Google," following her frustration with the constant question of why there aren't any Black women in this industry.

It is as clear as day for any ethical student and avid tech enthusiast the ideal Cashless Society is far from reality. Also clear is the fact we are accelerating innovations, designs, and architectural implementations designed by experts from mostly white demographics, excluding the cultural relevance, context, and contributions of the global majority of Black, Asian, Latinos, women, and BIPOC. As technology, like policy, has long-term implications, it is critical we hit pause, reflect, and restart from a place of shared values and collaboration, not the current exclusive and master mentality. For corporations to claim they are for humanity and inclusion and then spend resources derailing the very ethical research and contributions from excluded communities is contrary to the ideal Cashless Society we all aspire to. This Cashless Society is one in which representation matters and fairness, ownership, trust, and accessible scale are foundational.

For most excluded communities, the Gebru narrative is familiar. Great talent, time, and effort are sacrificed in well-meaning projects only to be derailed by racist, sexist, homophobic, and other patriarchal excuses followed by apologies to de better, with little to no meaningful change or impact. As stated, we only need to look at the colonial legacy of extractive economies and perhaps the American origins of free labor vs. slavery to understand the resistance to a more inclusive and transparent Cashless Society realization. It has become a *"myth"* that it costs more to do the right thing, according to Heritage.org, rather than saving future costs from violations, as explored by HuffPost. In corporate America, anything but the right thing is pursued, recognized, and rewarded, as seen by scandals in healthcare, data breaches, and financial crises, according to a *Forbes* report on ESG investing. What is right for Google need not necessarily translate into what is good for society, and yet it is individuals, not machines, making these critical decisions.

Following Timnit Gebru's departure from Google, *The Verge* reported Google's firing of a second AI ethics researcher following an internal investigation. The *WIRED* magazine was quick to highlight the exit of two Google AI researchers spurred more fallout. Indeed, the Google AI researchers laid out clear demands in solidarity with their colleagues under attack from Google and the scientific community, often a recipient of corporate funding for research would also back them. Historically and to date, private corporations fund academia research, and a few professors are beginning to say "no" to sponsorships in exchange for silence.

Part of this new movement is professors who are not attending Google-funded research conferences. The professors are also now piloting experimental research funding options both as a resistance and sustainable way forward to limit the biased influence of corporate cash on scientific and especially AI research in America and the world. This trend is nothing new, as evidenced by the oil, tobacco, and sugar industries that often fund research and/or lobbying in favor of their sectors in exchange for protection, both scientific and legal, against government scrutiny and particularly ethical violations investigations. *WIRED* acknowledges Gebru's exit from Google as a wedge that exposed the crisis in AI.

The December 16, 2021, letter from Google's ethical AI team to officials, including Google CEO Pichai, by Alex Hanna, Gebru's coworker, asks that Megan Kacholia, the company vice president, no longer be part of the team, adding, "We have lost trust in her as a team leader," according to Bloomberg. The letter argues, "Google's short-sighted decision to fire and retaliate against a core member of the ethical AI team makes it clear we need swift and structural changes if this work is to continue, and if the legitimacy of the field as a whole is to persevere…This research must be able to contest the company's short-term interests and immediate revenue agendas, as well as to investigate AI that is deployed by Google's competitors with similar ethical motives."

The researchers also asked for Google to offer Gebru a chance to return to the company at a "higher level" than she had before, with an apology from Kacholia, the vice president, and Jeff Dean, the AI division chief. Other demands mentioned in the letter are for Google to issue a public commitment to academic integrity and establish racial literacy training for management, something that fell on deaf ears with an anti-ethics and/or diversity equity and Inclusion federal mandate under the Trump administration. To see federal institutions support or signal a preference for racist and unethical business practices is beyond disappointing but also somewhat fundamentally American, as we have discussed the system history of some of these challenges in earlier chapters.

One can only admire the integrity of the Google ethical AI researchers for not only backing one of their own at the risk of losing their job and the cash affiliated with it but also for doing the right thing by the ideal ethical Cashless Society we aspire to. By standing up when those in power could not, individuals are once again demonstrating their power is guiding the human race to a more ethical and inclusive society despite systemic and institutional bias often exercised by poor unethical leadership and exclusive innovations.

"We study how AI ethics are being operationalized, and the biggest challenges we face are so much of the ethical AI conversation is happening behind closed doors, and so many voices are excluded from the AI ethics conversation. AI ethics needs more case studies—about successes and failures—from which to build common knowledge and improve practices across the industry and to

recognize the past and future contributions of community activists in addressing many of the most trenchant ethical issues for AI."

- DATA & SOCIETY RESEARCHER EMANUEL MOSS INTERVIEWED BY ALL TECH IS HUMAN.

On Friday, May 21, 2021, I received an invitation from a Canada|UK friend and colleague, Denis Nwanshi, the founder and director of NetraDigital Inc., asking me to deliver a lecture to undergraduate students at London South Bank University (LSBU) during their interuniversity hackathon themed: harnessing disruptive technologies for the post-COVID-19 era. According to the event flyer, "Hackathon teams are free to build business and consumer solutions based on artificial intelligence, machine learning, blockchain, natural language processing, APIs, cloud, mobile, data analytics, Internet of Things, robotic process automation (RPA), and other disruptive technologies." It is this kind of practical and experience-based learning that should be scaled across schools from primary school to higher education instead of the age-old and colonial theory memorization education system still haunting us in the twenty-first century. I am excited to engage these future leaders and innovators on conversations around medical supply chains, mobile e-commerce, money transfer, telemedicine, and COVID-19 patient care. With such curious, determined, and lifelong learner students, the ethical Cashless Society ideal is still a possibility, if only we can play our part to build it, use, regulate, and sustain it.

Since the Cashless Society refers to electronic transactions, whether it be for finance, health, education, transport, or service delivery, we can say most countries are still in transition to a Cashless Society. However, some cities, towns, enterprises, and even families are already living a Cashless Society lifestyle from Japan to some parts of China, the US, and Africa. Every time electronic or digital transactions are preferred or provided, even if cash is still an option, we can analyze that as a Cashless Society experience. It is easy to assume the inevitability of technology is the answer, but nothing could be further from the truth. Only ethically designed and human-first innovations can dynamically adapt to the needs of our species over time. Otherwise, the technology becomes irrelevant as our values evolve. Since culture is both relative and dynamic, i.e., it evolves, what is needed is an ethical and inclusive innovation framework that supports learning through feedback but also integrates the human values we aspire to celebrate and preserve. Activism changes policy and policy becomes law. There is work right now being done in legislative and judicial arms of government to move the needle toward inclusion and access that should not be taken for granted. Change is a marathon and it takes time. So, in the end, humans are the solution. In reality, we don't need to have all the answers today; we just need to acknowledge what's wrong and work toward solutions together. While the next few chapters capture what role we can all play, including both private and public institutions, we must never forget the fundamental truth: individual action and agency is the key to change. We must each reach for a better society, one that is more just, inclusive, and representative of our shared humanity across cultures and borders.

CHAPTER 10

THE POWER OF SHARED VALUE

"A ship in the harbor is safe, but that's not what ships are built for."

— UNKNOWN

I have learned some trial by fire lessons while transitioning from Wall Street to entrepreneurship and now management consulting in private equity. I have been lucky to engage both public and private institutions across the world over the last decade, and it is clear there is a fight for global dominance between the US and China. One such area is digital payments and regulatory compliance, with each country's companies being viewed as a national security threat. For example, my cofounder, Franco Abott, and I faced cross-border payments and funding challenges when launching and scaling the DreamGalaxy platform globally. This also had to do with the different anti-money laundering (AML) and know your customer (KYC) laws that surround funding often being favorable to US firms and less so to emerging market ventures and outflows. In the end, we decided to lead with the US holding company and a Kenya-based subsidiary for our global operations.

The China vs. US Internet division as a race to Cashless Society dominance and independence is as real as the Cold War and World Wars, except it is being fought in the court of public opinion using zeros and ones. A binary or divided Internet is not good for anyone, but a decentralized Internet ecosystem backed by blockchain. It might be, but only if we embed the human values of identity, ownership, trust, and scale. Global institutions, from the United Nations (UN) to the World Intellectual Property Organization (WIPO), seem to be comfortable with the status quo of racism, nationalism, and genocide-driven innovations and commercialization rather than pushing for and adapting an ethical Cashless Society based on mutual respect.

China is leading in global intellectual property (IP) registrations for patents and trademarks, especially in scientific research and technology innovation, according to WIPO Technology Trends 2021 report. This is both a result of long-term strategic commitment as well as a desire to play by the free market rules in a transitional style rather than a "Big Bang" switch, as is often the case for World Bank cash and mostly debt-funded efforts in emerging markets. By betting on strategic innovation and intellectual property, China is betting on itself and, in turn, on ownership in the only language the world understands—IP. This is contrary to the often-mandated projects that follow World Bank funds to emerging markets, despite those projects being against the very countries' agendas they are meant to help, as explored in detail in my first book, *The Last Digital Frontier*, or annual World Bank failure reports.

Ownership, both in the physical sense as well as the legal or intellectual sense, becomes a critical factor in the ethical implementation and sustainability of a Cashless Society. It is no wonder there is talk of a split Internet, one influenced by China and the other by the US and its allies, who each day seem more like China's allies in both business and strategy. A divided Internet, while already a reality in some countries such as North Korea's intranet and China's censored or regulated firewalls, would not bond well for global innovations and communication. As such, the decentralized nature of the Internet is likely to be sustained in the long term, albeit influenced by one superpower or another. This is unless the masses wake up and intentionally use and support only decentralized solutions, a rather impractical proposition. The US-China relations are likely to continue deteriorating as China seeks a mutual respect relationship with the West, something the US is yet to practice as the self-declared world police.

The digital ownership issue is even more of concern across Africa, where decades of extraction-based policies have rendered ownership and IP protection nearly obsolete. Foreign companies easily copy, steal, and deny local innovations while commercializing those same innovations locally and globally. Only when emerging markets' IP is enforced and commercialized equitably will the imbalance of power (both economic and political) be narrowed. The regional IP body, ARIPO, while well-intentioned, shrinks in comparison to filing data from China's IP, often indicating lifetime Africa filings are less than 10 percent of all global annual filings from countries like Germany, the US, or China, according to the WIPO Technology Trends report. According to the African Union, IP ownership and a shared value model are the missing link for an ethical Cashless Society across Africa. The African Union through Agenda 2063 is galvanizing a continent with 1.3 billion people, most of the world's natural resources, the world's youngest population with two-thirds under thirty years of age, and the largest mobile money market in the world, as highlighted on its website.

IP ownership shouldn't just be nice to have, but a required or core pillar strategy for the African Union, regional bodies, and individual countries, as well as its citizens. This is because the costly filing fees to register African IP and be recognized by Western or Asian countries are hindrances to innovation on the continent with no guarantee of enforcement or protection from the very countries with a history of stealing and profiting from African wealth, resources, and IP. Rather, the African Union and member states should develop their own centralized IP registration system, implement an intra-Africa IP enforcement policy and framework, and negotiate mutual respect as well as enforcement and recognition of Africa registered IP by the West, Asia, and Latin American countries. Only this reciprocal mutual IP acknowledgment and enforcement for commercialization framework, not a colonial mandated Western IP first framework, is likely to succeed and foster ethical innovations in the long term. The era of foreign subsidiaries carrying out innovation, research, and tests on the continent alongside, and often at the expense of Africans, only to turn, register, and commercialize that IP globally, including Africa, should be replaced by one in which African IP is registered by Africans and protected by countries against foreign trolls and copycats.

According to BBC, research shows most lawyers and innovators, including their board of directors, shy away from cross-border collaborations due to a lack of global cross-border IP enforcement, as seen by the Apple trademark loss in China as well as other pushbacks by local companies and countries against multinational brands. The recent India resistance against Amazon and Google and China's ban on Google Core Services use in China as just the smoking gun to the ethical dilemmas that will arise from ownership in a Cashless Society. If data is the new oil, then IP ownership is the new drilling right, and drillers will "drill, baby, drill" once those rights are secured.

In fact, more than anything, COVID-19 has exposed both the gaps and challenges of nationalist-driven innovation and protectionist policies, as highlighted by the EU vaccine rollout troubles. For example, the Oxford-AstraZeneca vaccine from the University of Oxford and a private company, AstraZeneca, faced commercial rollout huddles due to disagreements on IP and/or licensing and commercialization use cases between the university and private company. This is a contrast to an African rollout of COVID-Organics, the Madagascar African-made COVID-19 medical supplement that saw successes and expedited sharing of IP across African Union member countries despite global criticism from a lack of western-approved standardized vaccine trial approval process, as per the AFP. COVID-19 exposed the hypocrisy of Western science progress, in that most journalists and researchers alike were shocked Africa was largely spared by the pandemic despite its preventive health approach to healthcare with limited critical care hospital units and/or vaccine manufacturing capacity. In fact, the inequity around IP sharing and licensing is no different from the US capitalization of the AIDS vaccine market, often discouraging purchases from other innovators like India, according to *The Washington Post*. Moreover, both Yale and Brookings studies highlight how cash drives the preference for AIDS drugs over vaccines from a profit maximization model. As such, emerging market innovations have historically been sidelined by Western markets' geopolitics and nationalist trade agendas.

As if wishing COVID-19 on such a struggling continent was not enough insult, any attempts by Africans to pilot and distribute locally designed and tested health supplements and vaccines was despised and/or sabotaged from an IP conflict issue. Such was the case of the Ugandan-made vaccine, Covidex, from Mbarara University of Science and Technology (MUST) in 2021. According to the *Daily Monitor*, a leading independent newspaper in Uganda, sources at the institution revealed the deepening rift between MUST and Professor Patrick Ogwang over Covidex had at its center, work spats, use of a seven-million-dollar (24.6-billion-shilling) grant, and expectations of a windfall from brisk sales of the new drug. Monitor adds some critics said the Uganda National Drug Authority (NDA) favors or is manipulated by pharmaceutical companies and foreign investors who don't want to see development in herbal medicines.

The new leverage of COVID-19 vaccines for soft power diplomacy from Russia, China, and now the US means global priorities are not about global health, but rather the value exchange doses can bring in terms of allies and/or negotiated arrangements. Here is a perfect philosophical and practical example of a cashless transaction in the literal sense without digital payments but rather with the vaccine as the bartered service. The ethics around who gets to live and when are definitely tied to the ownership of the IP and the related innovations or distribution channels.

Despite lackluster ethical AI and inclusive innovation activism across the US and the enforcement of EU data privacy laws, there is a general consensus that not enough is being done to foster inclusive innovation, and groups have sprung up in Europe and the US to challenge what they view as the rising power of Silicon Valley, with the advocacy largely centered on privacy issues. Foxglove, for example, a nonprofit with a budget this year of just over a half-million dollars, has cut a different path, taking aim at government-created algorithms that increasingly make decisions in civic areas like education and immigration, according to *The Wall Street Journal*. "There was almost nobody in civil society doing anything about that," said one of Foxglove's founders, Cori Crider, a thirty-nine-year-old Texan. The four-woman group adds, "What we're interested in is this change in the way power has been exercised, almost hiding a bunch of contestable policy judgments behind a technical veneer." *The Wall Street Journal* concludes Foxglove is now looking into tech worker rights.

Data and Society Research Institute's analysis and research bring a whole new perspective to navigating issues of identity, ownership, trust, and scale in a Cashless Society. Beyond ethical AI experts and/or regulations and ethical leadership, which seems to be lacking, the court of public opinion is winning the day for now.

> *"Outside pressure does have an impact. People told us trusted civil society organizations with good research and information can affect change. Regulators, either threatening or enacting regulation, also provoke change. Similarly, media attention, particularly negative media attention, can also shape policies inside companies."*
>
> - DATA AND SOCIETY HEALTH AND DATA PROGRAM DIRECTOR AMANDA LENHART, DATABITE NO. 143.

Such outside pressure is what Facebook has to deal with following recent rulings from the EU data privacy courts that advocate for the separation of EU residents' data vs. the non-EU residents' data, such as US customers or users. To comply, Facebook would likely have to reengineer its service to silo off most data it collects from European users, or stop serving them entirely, at least temporarily, according to *The Wall Street Journal*. *The Wall Street Journal* added in a security filing this year Facebook said applying the regulator's decision would "materially and adversely affect our business, financial condition, and results of operations." These regulatory and activist-driven calls for change cut across borders and industries from China to Africa and from technology or healthcare to finance, as shared by Janet Yellen on Twitter.

In her tweet from April 5, 2021, Janet Yellen, the US Secretary of the Treasury, references a need to go back to a US policy that is in line with US values but falls short of highlighting those values and their relevance to the global majority, especially those in emerging markets. American influence during the world wars goes without credit, especially to those in Europe who were saved by this young, ambitious, and innovative nation from the brink of collapse. For the rest of the world, however—particularly Africa and, by extension, all former European and/or Western colonies, including US slave holding ports and territories—the growing influence of the US has not always been a good thing. My position is not anti-America, as today's self-declared "US patriots" might claim, but rather one of a critic, based on our shared human history and facts.

As someone who grew up in Uganda, East Africa, I aspire to America's ideals and values despite the illusionary and often conflicting reality of being "Black in America" and, indeed, the world. Needless to say, I can understand Janet Yellen's call to embrace American idealism and practically transfer it into bold, forward-looking, inclusive policies that would get the US out of the current crisis while creating a sustainable coexistence with its neighbors and global partners. For Janet, and many of us, it is clear an authoritative, self-centered, and expansionist US policy is unsustainable in the twenty-first century. Rather, a decentralized and inclusive framework that captures, defends, and scales American ideals and values in alignment with its global neighbors and the emerging markets is the right way forward, and the work cannot wait any longer to begin.

FROM VALUES TO ACTION: ACTUALIZING THE ETHICAL CASHLESS SOCIETY IDEA

One of the 2020/2021 FinTech and data or cybersecurity innovations is Middesk's flagship identity product used by banks and financial service companies like Plaid to help small businesses more easily obtain services like a bank account or credit card. While traditional databases in this space can date back to the 1800s, Middesk provides a more up-to-date database on potential company clients, including incorporation documents and tax identification numbers from more than seventy-five million businesses, according to *Forbes*. Middesk's revenue grew by five times last year, Mack said to *Forbes*, though he declined to share specifics. *Forbes* added this growth prompted the start-up to raise a sixteen-million-dollar Series A round led by Sequoia with participation from Accel and Y Combinator, bringing its total fundraising to twenty million dollars.

The rise is due to the increasing power of digital innovation, particularly digital banking, to deliver meaningful, ethical, and inclusive access to millions of unbanked globally, especially the US. Traditional banks, beholden to a cash-based society and a paper-based identity verification system often based on racially biased historical data like credit scores and redlining zip codes to exclude Black and minority citizens from loans and other financial services, are getting a run for their money from upstarts and digital banking firms like Middesk and SoFi, as reported in *Forbes*. In a dog-eat-dog world of American capitalism, where it is literally an adapt-or-die reality, there is pressure for banks to not only digitize but to boldly embrace the very technologies like blockchain and cryptocurrencies they have spent decades and millions of dollars lobbying against.

The future is digital, cashless, contactless, and traditional banks are not ready. Companies like Square, founded by Twitter CEO and founder Jack Dorsey to create and print receipts on demand for small businesses, are scaling into digital banking through their Cash App platform that powers a debit card, direct deposit, or routing transfers and recently investing in both stocks and cryptocurrencies. CNBC reports Square's success has drawn the envy of existing players like PayPal, owners of Braintree, as well as other money transfer services to also support cryptocurrency trading and digital wallets for its millions of users globally. According to Bloomberg, competition is good in that companies compete to make the user happy both from a service delivery—e.g., speed of transaction—and security, or data privacy, point of view. This is happening despite a lack of a clear US support and/or policy toward tokenization, cryptocurrencies, and/or a digital federal reserve and the growing adoption of blockchain and cryptocurrencies by US firms to respond to foreign and local interest, use, and scale of Cashless Society solutions despite US government and legislature (congress and senate) reluctance to offer clear investment and tax policy.

This is an indication the US risk-based innovation is not immune to the decentralized demands of billions of global citizens who feel underserved and excluded from the colonial and post-World War II cash-based US dollar institutions.

Perhaps, Bank of America should rebrand to Bitcoin of America as many cash-hungry firms did in the early 2010s by adding blockchain to their corporate name to raise money as investors were looking for blockchain innovations to invest in. If, according to American icon and film character Gordon Gekko from the film *Greed*, greed is good and will save capitalism, then the US and its institutions must wake and realize the changing tide powered by a lack of trust in the status quo and follow the money which, in this case, is the digital currency powering a Cashless Society revolution across the US and globally.

This transition, like the US transition from fossil fuels and coal to renewable energy is critical for America's sustainable energy and financial independence. After all, America is one of China's largest trading partners and creditors—over US 1.063 trillion dollars, the US Treasury reported to Congress in April 2021. The US, in turn, owes US debt and could, in fact, down the road, be mandated to pay for Chinese trade and imports in China's own digital reserve currency launched this year. With China's increasing influence and global partners through its Belt and Road Initiative, there is reason for the US to not blink when it comes to adopting and implementing an ethical, trust-based Cashless Society.

American values and ideals, including democracy, are at stake when trust is undermined and, more importantly, restored by a trustless counterparty or decentralized finance alternatives like the ever-in-demand DeFi platforms and coins, e.g., Binance. Stakeholder capitalism vs. shareholder capitalism diminishes others over shareholders. One hundred percent of bankers from the largest six US banks would not support employees' formation of unions when asked by Representative Sherrod Brown during a congressional testimony session on May 26, 2021, streamed on Bloomberg TV. The testimonies showed how financial institutions and big tech are willing to defy any conversations around ethics, fairness, and/or workers' rights and increased compensation, i.e., the living wage and equal pay for women and/or underrepresented groups. Cryptocurrency or blockchain allows for tokenization, i.e., partial ownership via utility tokens, which can allow employees and partners to be part-owners in ecosystems and companies in a more direct and sustainable way where they are active participants and beneficiaries of their work and input. A good example is the Chobani yogurt brand employees as owners model if it was then tokenized or digitized. NPR reported in April 2016 that Chobani CEO Hamdi Ulukaya gave employees stock certificates in a piece titled "Why Chobani Gave Employees a Financial Stake In Company's Future." According to NPR, Corey Rosen of the National Center for Employee Ownership says employee ownership takes many different forms, and in a growing number of companies, workers own the firms outright. NPR reports that the dairy company Schreiber Foods, for example, is larger than Chobani and is 100 percent employee-owned through an employee stock ownership plan, or ESOP. Corey Rosen is quoted by NPR as saying that about 10% of US companies now have some sort of ESOP that allows employees to own, control and share in the profits of a company through a trust because they enjoy large tax benefits and because retiring baby boomers who own companies see it as a good way to transfer ownership.

The classic use case of Doctor AI in healthcare is where the physician saves 80 percent of the manual or repetitive tasks, like filing and clerical work, to instead focus on human-centered service delivery to patients in and out of the hospital. The concern of Doctor AI's fully replacing humans while a possibility is still far off with concerns around autonomy in decision-making, authoring in diagnosis, as well as the ultimate liability risk from the automated practice and healthcare delivery. So, if doctors can't be held accountable, should accountability shift to the AI system? Just because AI systems can't currently be held liable for their decisions, that shouldn't stop efforts to incorporate some form of moral responsibility into AI systems. Tigard emphasized AI is designed to evolve. "We're talking about things made to learn…Let's teach," said Tigard from Yale School of Medicine. It's yet to be known whether AI can be taught to make moral decisions that depend on empathy and semantic understanding and Elon Musk's Neuralink, a brain chip implant for increase cognize simulation and computation is a likely first stage of the hybrid human-machine interactions that may be the foundation for such analysis.

Columbia University student Ima Chimo interviewed Nunu Ntshingila, Facebook Africa CEO, at the African Economic Forum 2021 virtual event, which I attended virtually via Zoom, and we were fortunate to ask a few questions as the audience. Nunu acknowledges Facebook's impact and scale in a COVID-19 and post-COVID-19 world where:

- Partnerships are critical, e.g., the ability to spread education (not miseducation) across the platform

- Connectivity allows for education beyond physical spaces (and across borders)

- Schools, universities, and businesses can easily connect and trade online, and the Facebook ecosystem is the fastest way to enable connection and businesses to have an African and global platform

The Facebook Africa CEO did not ignore the challenges of trying to bring Africa to the world, especially youth impacting political issues such as #EndSARSNigeria protest censorships and the 2020 presidential election in Uganda sharing:

- At the heart are community standards meant to keep people safe and do not create harm. Since 2016, we have tripled the size of people working on what safety looks like, including localizing African languages like Zulu and Housa.

- On misinformation, we work with eighty independent fact-checkers and in Africa, across twenty languages, so the information found is correct. We go as far as removing content, adding warnings, or removing people.

- We have created so many tools to make sure political information is safe. We take down content from bad actors or others who violate our standards.

- On #EndSARS, what happened shouldn't have. We have to automate tools to flag content; some were incorrectly flagged during the #EndSARS campaign and we reversed it. We need more manual flagging and retraining algorithms and employees to guard against such flagging. Information should have never been brought down.

- For Uganda, we have a huge public policy against such, and pages were taken down even when Facebook was shut down by the government. Everyone has a voice on our platform, but unfortunately, Facebook was shut down because that was the feeling at that time. We believe all voices should be heard.

On ethical and authentic leadership, Nunu shares she knew she could not find the voice of my male predecessors, so she started finding her own way, understanding who she was so she could bring her authentic self. She said human capital development is her passion.

> "Ultimately, it's about people...on building talent. How do I make sure Africa thrives in the future and how do I find my voice, which is a female voice, that can be understood and accepted around the world?"
>
> NUNU, FACEBOOK AFRICA CEO

Sheida A. Chumba remarked the collective African market is yet to actively begin calling out for users' privacy rights, say like in the EU and USA. The Facebook Africa CEO reiterated Facebook's primary goal is to make sure people have access, and the second is about creating both public, like Facebook and Instagram, as well as private platforms, like WhatsApp and Messenger, with end-to-end encryption. Nunu concludes, "As tech companies, we need to create tools for users to enable them to choose tech bubbles they need to feel secure while allowing seamless movement from public to private forums." Entire countries are being banned or excluded on social media by retaliatory governments or presidents, such as the June 2021 Twitter ban of Nigerian president Muhammadu Buhari after he posted public endangering remarks, according to Brookings. Buhari retaliated by banning Twitter from Nigeria, impacting millions of business, nonprofit, government, and private citizen accounts. This is no different from US President Trump's push to ban Chinese-owned TikTok, among other platforms, as retaliation. Private institutions have a shared value responsibility to implement ethical policies that sustain and do not violate freedom of speech and other fundamental rights. "If it was authoritarian to ban Twitter, it was even more problematic for an American in Silicon Valley to poke their finger in the affairs of a sovereign state," says Adaobi Tricia Nwaubani, a Nigerian novelist, to BBC.

CHAPTER 11

THE POWER OF SHARED RESPONSIBILITY

"The greater the power a civilization wields in the world, the less capable its thinkers may be to recognize the naivete of their own beliefs. Humanity can do better."
- SUSAN BUCK-MORSS (HEGEL, HAITI, AND UNIVERSAL HISTORY).

African billionaire and Africapitalist Tony Elumelu on Africa Day 2021 hosted a conversation livestreamed on YouTube with panelists H.E. Paul Kagame, president of the Republic of Rwanda; Dr. Ngozi Okonjo-Iweala, director-general (DG) of the World Trade Organization (WTO); Dr. Tedros Adhanom Ghebreyesus, DG of the World Health Organization (WHO); and Makhtar Diop, managing director (MD) of the International Finance Corporation (IFC). It was an insightful meeting dissecting the issues of Western racial apartheid, export-driven innovation, lack of ethical leadership, and inclusive or accessible innovation we (Africa) face as a continent and creating action plans to address them. Mr. Kagame called out the West on their "racial apartheid and genocide policies," as evidenced by COVID-19 vaccine debates as well as foreign policy, and asked African leaders to do more for their people while seeking mutual respect from non-Africans.

Dr. Ngozi pledged to offer the WTO support for any actionable intra-Africa agenda policies, especially around manufacturing and the Africa Continental Free Trade Area (AfCFTA). Despite being dismissed by world leaders, Dr. Tedros reaffirmed his initial pledge to share the vaccine equitably rather than use it as a genocide or tyrant negotiation tool to secure the global health of all of us. Makhtar, humble as always, shared many talented Africans could be serving in his position if only they had access to the opportunity and promised to continue challenging the IFC to present practical programs that support intra-Africa, not just export trade, especially in realizing the potential for a single African Market, as per the AfCFTA. According to Tony Elumelu, Africa's biggest assets are its youth and time to engage them to aid our economic recovery.

The Africa challenge for the West is no different from China's ask for a world of shared values based on mutual respect, not the West's superiority complex. "Regrettably, simply because of the obstruction of one country, the Security Council hasn't been able to speak with one voice," Chinese foreign minister Wang Yi said during the virtual meeting to discuss the Israel-Palestine conflict and recent May 2021 escalations, as reported by *The Wall Street Journal*. He added, "We call upon the United States to shoulder its due responsibilities of taking a just position."

Recently, the US, a self-declared cop of the world, has increasingly fallen short of delivering the ethical leadership and inclusive innovations the world expects. Instead, there is more of a nationalist and inward focus.

> "I want to thank the gentleman from New York and the other Republicans who are supporting this for their bipartisanship. To the other 90 percent of our friends on the other side of the aisle, holy cow. Incoherence, no idea what you're talking about. Benghazi, you guys chased the former secretary of state all over the country, spent millions of dollars. We have people scaling the Capitol, hitting the Capitol Police with lead pipes across the head, and we can't get bipartisanship. What else has to happen in this country? Cops. This is a slap in the face to every rank-and-file cop in the United States. If we're going to take on China, if we're going to rebuild the country, if we're going to reverse climate change, we need two

political parties in this country that are both living in reality, and you ain't one of them."

- DEMOCRATIC CONGRESSMAN TIM RYAN OF OHIO, MAY 19, 2021, ON THE 175 REPUBLICAN HOUSE MEMBERS, INCLUDING HOUSE REPUBLICAN LEADER KEVIN MCCARTHY, WHO VOTED AGAINST CREATING A TEN-MEMBER COMMISSION TO INVESTIGATE THE JANUARY 6 INSURRECTION.

Europe, both East and West, is also lacking in delivering the ethical leadership and policies critical to the Cashless Society. The World Business Angels Investment Forum (WBAF) at the Europe Summit on February 16, 2021, centered around discussions about investors' role in topics such as furthering digital and financial inclusion, encouraging female entrepreneurship, and economic growth. Attendee Kevin Hin summarizes ten key takeaways from the WBAF Summit:

1. Europe needs to work together to erase barriers.

2. Policy changes need to be made at local, national, and multi-national levels.

3. Switching to the green economy mindset is vital.

4. Education and nurturing entrepreneurial spirit and ecosystem are important.

5. European values and ethics can help entrepreneurs excel.

6. Empowering women with investment is important.

7. Flexibility around companies.

8. Creating value encourages sustainable growth.

9. Innovation is essential for European progression.

10. The importance of public/private partnerships increased in pandemic times.

According to a Data & Society Research Institute newsletter titled *Data and Society,* Daniel Tigard is a Senior Research Associate in the Institute for History & Ethics of Medicine at the Technical University of Munich, Germany. His current work addresses issues of moral responsibility in emerging technology. He taught a summer course at Yale's ICB on moral distress in medicine and explains that American society shifted only recently from the model of "doctors know best" to "patients know best." "Now we're seeing a new shift," he said, "where machines seem to 'know' best."

"As medicine devolves into a world driven by AI, much of a doctor's autonomy or decision-making responsibilities may be transferred to AI systems," said Joseph Carvalko, BSEE, JD, chair of the Technology and Ethics Working Research Group at Yale's ICB featured in the data, AI, and society newsletter. Carvalko thinks doctors will increasingly be pressured to hand over authority to AI technologies and potentially become legally accountable for overriding the decision of a machine using the latest technology. At issue, as raised earlier, is whether doctors would feel comfortable overriding and going against the algorithm's logical decision or whether the machine would have veto power of the empathetic yet sometimes biased human decision. The question of whether it's ethical just to hold humans accountable for AI decisions and their implications is far from clear when it comes to accountability, responsibility, culpability, and liability.

Tigard explained traditional legal liability depends on moral autonomy, a condition that relies on factors doctors normally possess as knowledge and control. But it's not always clear how AI systems make decisions, and there is an increasing trend to push for explainable AI and whether humans are capable of understanding complex AI decision-making. Rather, would simple human explanations suffice and help us manage our fear of automation since technical or bot-specific explanations may be overwhelming or lack a human context?

Dr. Jose Morey, who I interviewed for this book in 2021, offered by far the most extensive insight on how both private and public institutions can deliver ethical leadership and inclusive innovations for the Cashless Society. When asked, "What does cashless society mean to you…and are we there yet?" Dr. Jose responded, "We're not there yet, but we are close. Now you're seeing more and more big players get into digital economy." He acknowledged the rise in innovation from emerging markets like China, India, and Africa and the global, decolonial questions: "Should the US lead? Do they have the moral foundations to?"

Dr. Jose states, "One of the things we will always lead in is compared to the rest of the world, we are really the best experiment when it comes to a heterogeneous society. I mean, there is no one who is more of a melting pot than the United States...always competing. But if we don't, if we don't use our strength, and if we try to kill each other over our strength, we will ultimately lose." He argues rather than exporting or mandating US exceptionalism, the US should share lessons learned from its great experiment, leaving the locals autonomy to pick, adapt, and use what may work for them on their own terms.

He adds that America as a whole, hopefully, can be more open in certain sectors by being honest about their mistakes and saying, "Hey, this is where we messed up and we are trying to fix it. Yeah, we're not perfect...Take what you want, integrate it locally, put your flavor on it, and then create something new from it." He honestly thinks that's where the US can always lead because the US is such a multicultural society. While neoliberalism and multiculturalism have not always delivered authentic and meaningful change to those traditionally excluded and marginalized, there is value and wisdom in Dr. Jose's arguments. For example, he defends his position by adding, "I know that is scary to a lot of people, and there's a lot of fight against it, but if we own it, I think multiculturalism is the means by which we can help the rest of the world grow, because we can say, 'Hey, we've taken components from your culture and we've included into ours. That's been good and bad for us and here's why.'" He ends with an acknowledgment the US is a great experiment, and like entrepreneurship, some experiments succeed and some experiments fail.

While Massachusetts isn't the first to propose legislation about facial recognition technology, it's now home to Bill H.117 that would penalize companies that misuse such tech via hefty fines and sanctions enforced by the state attorney general's office, according to GovTech. The bill, according to Representative Dylan Fernandes, would prevent companies from sharing customers' data without their consent as a way to protect individuals from financial, physical, or reputational harm. Examples of actions the legislation would punish include:

- Selling customer data to third parties

- Scanning data to discriminate against customers

- Using data in a way that would legally impact a customer's financial status, housing, or employment situation

Despite having seen similar bills, Fernandes said, "…This one is different because it places regulations on companies to ensure they don't actively harm or engage in unfair client practices by using facial recognition data in a harmful way." He said the bill would allow citizens to submit a complaint to the attorney general's office to enforce the regulations similar to the recent anti-abortion bill and legislation incentivizing citizen reports or tips. "This bill gives the AG's office regulation drafting and enforcement authority over facial recognition technology and data," a spokesperson from the office said via email, cautioning, "Since the bill has not passed yet, it's too early to predict which division or bureau would handle this at this specific time," according to GovTech.

US Senate committee leaders have drafted a 110-billion-dollar compromise measure for basic and advanced technology research and science over five years and the creation of a White House chief manufacturing officer in the face of rising competitive pressure from China, according to a copy of the 131-page draft legislation seen in 2021 by Reuters. The increasing reality of a Cashless Society founded on AI, quantum computing, and BioTech innovations in Asian countries like China, South Korea, Japan, and Singapore is waking the US to not only update its policy but also put money where its mouth is, i.e., invest in ethical leadership programs and inclusive innovations. These efforts are unfortunately likely to fail or have minimal impact if there is an exclusionary national security rationale behind such limited application of innovation as opposed to borderless solutions that scale and are accessible globally. According to VentureBeat, the draft bill would also block Chinese companies from participating in the Manufacturing USA program without a waiver. VentureBeat concludes the program is a government- and company-led effort to build up industrial competitiveness, cut energy use, and strengthen US national security.

Beyond the policy and regulatory innovations above, a keynote address from Dr. Albert Zeufack hosted by Columbia University's Séléna Batchily on Monday, March 22, from 12:45 p.m. to 2:00 p.m. ET, brought me insights on the role of affordable and sustainable energy beyond solar in scaling a Cashless Society. Dr. Zeufack is a Cameroonian national and the World Bank's Chief economist for Africa. The right regulatory environment, as seen by Kenya in East Africa vs. no support in West Africa, is a clear indicator of the need for allowing digital innovation to take place. According to Dr. Albert Zeufack in his keynote address during the March 22, 2021, African Economic Forum, learning from each other is the strong foundation humanity needs in Africa and the world.

One such area is how large-scale government innovation can be financed. Here, he further argues African countries are getting into debt distress, i.e., from liquidity to a solvency problem, with countries like Zambia defaulting on debt, especially due to COVID-19. The solution, according to Dr. Albert, is to avoid debt suspension schemes that often signal the beginning of defaulting to debt markets and moving from temporary solutions to more permanent and long-term solutions. The IMF Special Drawing Rights (SDRs) based on individual country contributions are not enough, and focus needs to be on bringing the private sector to the table with manageable rates. Making foreign currency accessible to local businesses, however, is still a challenge due to corruption.

Catherine Mendeley then asked Dr. Albert, "How do we navigate the bureaucracy of corrupt governments?"

Dr. Albert responded, "There is no private sector without an efficient public sector, as per my experience in Southeast Asia like Singapore and Malaysia. Let's try not to find ways to navigate but, rather, combat corruption, e.g., digital innovation tools which youth probably know better, as well as civil society engagement. It is the youths' responsibility to use tools and data to hold the government accountable."

When I had my opportunity, I asked Dr. Albert, "Can the AU issue a mandate for digital African passports and IDs and subsequently accelerate cross-border trade and payments via AfCFTA, as we, the youth, are tired of the lack of long-term vision and execution?"

Dr. Albert shared he completely agreed with what I had just said. He clarified, "Whenever I travel to African countries with non-African colleagues, a number of countries still require visas, and I am often the last one to go through the line. AfCFTA will tremendously benefit from an African passport being issued to all, even better if it is a digital passport. The current slow start for diplomats is for those who don't need it, but the youth urgently need digital passports."

These digital passports can then be leveraged to power digital wallets and mobile payments ecosystems like M-PESA. Such is the earlier shared example of Flutterwave partnering with PayPal to address its failure to include Africa in its cashless ambition. Safaricom's M-PESA leads the world from East Africa in mobile money (MoMo) transactions used by over 75 percent of the population and increasingly threatening traditional banks. PayPal, despite global dominance ambitions, has failed Africa, a continent of 1.3 billion people, and the Flutterwave partnership with PayPal is to help African merchants accept PayPal across borders.

In her book, *Hegel, Haiti, and Universal History,* Susan Buck-Morss, fully aware cultural racism has yet to be resolved, concludes:

"The mutual recognition between past and present that can liberate us from the recurring cycle of victim and aggressor...is a task of excavation that takes place not across

> *national boundaries, but without them. Its richest finds are at the edge of culture. Universal humanity is visible at the edges."*
>
> — SUSAN IN HER BOOK HEGEL, HAITI, AND UNIVERSAL HISTORY [P.150–151]

This continuous universal humanity experiment can be best guided by ethical leadership and inclusive innovation. On May 27, 2021, from Kigali, Rwanda, the Rwandan president and former African Union chairman, Paul Kagame, met with France's president, Emmanuel Macron. Macron took the unpopular and risky bet, to tell the truth, according to Rwanda and what we in Africa knew as reported by AfricaNews.com. It is a truth the West would prefer was swept under the rug—in particular, the role of France in the genocide in Rwanda. Kagame likened racism to genocide mentality that wipes out communities globally and instead urged for a future filled with mutual respect, not the superiority complex from the West that is the root cause of most global conflicts. May the Cashless Society of the future be built, run, and sustained on the fundamental belief all human beings are equal, i.e., Ubuntu. Kagame captured what I have struggled to grasp all my life with an answer to my curiosity on doing the right thing:

> *"Speaking the truth is risky. But you do it because it is right, even when it costs you something, even when it is*

unpopular. Despite some loud noises and voices, President Macron took this step. Politically and morally, this was an act of tremendous courage."

H.E. PAUL KAGAME, PRESIDENT OF RWANDA

May we live, learn, question, and act with courage in all we do. Our lives, our future, and our histories depend on it!

ACKNOWLEDGMENTS

It takes a village to raise a child, and this book is a result of the support from the following village or Cashless Society tribe.

Book presale supporters and author community members:

Robert Marrocco	Michele Harley
Colin Serling	Jan Renner
Rentsenkhand Enkh-Amgalan	Jeanette Elizabeth Hedberg Asai
Franco Abott	Eric Koester
Izabel D. Gomes	Karen Kemirembe
Nargiz Guliyeva	Patricia Tomanelli
Paul Caron	Evelyn Djoewanda
Hillary Woodward	Christopher Dokai
Cinthia Menutole	Mary Peng
Charlene Sebastian	Lauren Sullivan

Interview contributors: Naddine Rangger; Dr. Reid Blackman, PhD; Dr. Jose Morey; and others from BigTech to public institutions and activists.

Editors Natalie Lucas (DE), Vivian Rose (MRE), and many more from the New Degree Press community.

Early readers and @brianasingia digital denizens.

Press and early book praise from podcasts to TV and radio hosts as showcased on the author website: brianasingia.com.

Cashless Society 101 redefines "cashless society" beyond electronic transactions, digital currencies, flying cars, or connected devices to a human-first, ethical, and inclusive future that is both accessible and reflective of our individual uniqueness as well as shared diversity. May our thoughts become words, ideas become actions, actions become habits, habits become character, and character becomes values toward an inclusive, innovative society.

APPENDIX

INTRODUCTION

"Cashless." Cambridge English Dictionary. Accessed October 8, 2021. https://dictionary.cambridge.org/us/dictionary/english/cashless.

Cutter, Chip, Suzanne Vranica, and Alison Sider. "With Georgia Voting Law, the Business of Business Becomes Politics." The Wall Street Journal, April 10, 2021. https://www.wsj.com/articles/with-georgia-voting-law-the-business-of-business-becomes-politics-11618027250?mod=mhp.

Metz, Cade. "Who Is Making Sure the A.I. Machines Aren't Racist?" The New York Times, March 15, 2021. https://www.nytimes.com/2021/03/15/technology/artificial-intelligence-google-bias.html.

Ryan-Mosley, Tate. "Beauty Filters Are Changing the Way Young Girls See Themselves." MIT Technology Review, April 2, 2021. https://technologyreview.us11.list-manage.com/track/click?u=47c1a9cec9749a8f8cbc83e78&id=31196af806&e=819b58a375.

Semuels, Alana. "Machines and Ai Are Taking over Jobs Lost to Coronavirus." Time, August 6, 2020. https://time.com/5876604/machines-jobs-coronavirus/

CHAPTER 1

Achebe, Chinua and Anthony Appiah. *The African Trilogy: Things Fall Apart; Arrow of God; No Longer at Ease.* New York: Penguin Books, 2017.

Achebe, Chinua. *Things Fall Apart.* New York: Penguin Publishing Group, 2019.

Bureau, US Census. "Local Population Changes and Nation's Racial and Ethnic Diversity." The United States Census Bureau, August 17, 2021. https://www.census.gov/newsroom/press-releases/2021/population-changes-nations-diversity.html.

Conrad, Joseph, Owen Knowles, and Robert Hampson. *Heart of Darkness.* London: Penguin Books, 2007.

DiAngelo, Robin J. *White Fragility: Why It's so Hard for White People to Talk about Racism*. Boston: Beacon Press, 2020.

"Federal Circuit Upholds Attorneys' Fees Award, Grants Appellate Fees and Double Costs in Cheekd Dating App Case." IPWatchdog.com, March 23, 2021. https://www.ipwatchdog.com/2021/03/24/federal-circuit-upholds-attorneys-fees-award-grants-appellate-fees-and-double-costs-in-cheekd-dating-app-case/id=131314/.

"How Mickey Mouse Evades the Public Domain." Priceonomics. Accessed October 9, 2021. https://priceonomics.com/how-mickey-mouse-evades-the-public-domain/.

Norbrook, Nicholas, and Patrick Smith. "President Paul Kagame: 'Africa Has Been Struggling to Follow the West, and Now That System Is Crumbling.'" The Africa Report, July 9, 2019. https://www.theafricareport.com/15102/president-paul-kagame-africa-has-been-struggling-to-follow-the-west-and-now-that-system-is-crumbling/.

"The Origin of the LAPD Motto." Los Angeles Police Department. Accessed October 9, 2021. https://www.lapdonline.org/history_of_the_lapd/content_basic_view/1128.

Scott, Eugene. "Analysis | in Reference to 'Animals,' Trump Evokes an Ugly History of Dehumanization." The Washington Post, April 28, 2019. https://www.washingtonpost.com/news/the-fix/wp/2018/05/16/trumps-animals-comment-on-undocumented-immigrants-earn-backlash-historical-comparisons/.

"Supreme Court of the United States." SupremeCourt.gov. Accessed October 9, 2021. https://www.supremecourt.gov/opinions/20pdf/18-956_d18f.pdf.

Tadlock, Justin. "Upcoming Changes and Steps for an Overhauled WordPress Theme Review System." WP Tavern, March 19, 2021. https://wptavern.com/upcoming-changes-and-steps-for-an-overhauled-wordpress-theme-review-system.

Totenberg, Nina. "Supreme Court Hands Google a Win over Oracle in Multibillion-Dollar Case." NPR, April 5, 2021. https://www.npr.org/2021/04/05/984442325/supreme-court-hands-google-a-win-over-oracle-in-multibillion-dollar-case.

"The US-China Trade War: A Timeline." China Briefing News, March 22, 2021. https://www.china-briefing.com/news/the-us-china-trade-war-a-timeline/.

"World Intellectual Property Indicators Report: Trademark and Industrial Design Filing Activity Rose in 2019; Patent Applications Marked Rare Decline." WIPO. Accessed October 9, 2021. https://www.wipo.int/pressroom/en/articles/2020/article_0027.html.

Yu, Hua. *Shi Ge Ci Hui Li De Zhongguo = China in Ten Words*. Taibei Shi: Mai tian chu ban, 2010.

Africa Archives(@Africa_Archives). "If the Owners of the Natural Resources Go around Begging, Then You Should Know There's Something Wrong with Their Minds." President Kagame's Twitter, September 12, 2021. 5:41 AM. https://twitter.com/africa_archives/status/1437003447002443783?lang=bg.

CHAPTER 2

"Agenda 2063: The Africa We Want." African Union, January 1, 2019.
https://au.int/en/agenda2063/overview.

"Apple Loses China Trademark Case for 'iPhone' on Leather Goods." Reuters, May 4, 2016.
https://www.reuters.com/article/us-apple-china/apple-loses-china-trademark-case-for-iphone-on-leather-goods-idUSKCN0XV0YH.

Aryan, Aashish. "Explained: What the Jio Deal Means for Reliance and Facebook." The Indian Express, April 23, 2020.
https://indianexpress.com/article/explained/what-the-jio-deal-means-for-reliance-facebook-6374686/.

Ayer, A. J. *Bertrand Russell*. New York: The Viking Press, 1972.

Bright, Jake. "The Potential Problems and Profits for Netflix in Africa." TechCrunch, January 18, 2016.
https://techcrunch.com/2016/01/18/the-potential-problems-and-profits-for-netflix-in-africa/.

Byford, Sam. "Facebook Takes $5.7 Billion Stake in Indian Internet Giant Jio." The Verge, April 22, 2020.
https://www.theverge.com/2020/4/21/21230643/facebook-reliance-jio-investment-stake-whatsapp.

Canal, Stephane. "Africa: Analyzing Netflix's Attempts to Tap the African Market." allAfrica.com, September 29, 2021.
https://allafrica.com/stories/202109290156.html.

Conrad, Joseph. *Joseph Conrad's Heart of Darkness*. New York: W W Norton, 2020.

Cutter, Chip, Suzanne Vranica, and Alison Sider. "With Georgia Voting Law, the Business of Business Becomes Politics." The Wall Street Journal, April 10, 2021.
https://www.wsj.com/articles/with-georgia-voting-law-the-business-of-business-becomes-politics-11618027250.

Domonoske, Camila, and Alina Selyukh. "Why Apple Says It Won't Help Unlock That IPhone, in 5 Key Quotes." NPR, February 25, 2016.
https://www.npr.org/sections/thetwo-way/2016/02/25/468158520/why-apple-says-it-wont-help-unlock-that-iphone-in-5-key-quotes.

AT Editor. "Report: Kenya's Wind, Morocco's Solar Lead Africa on Clean Energy." Africa Times, May 6, 2021.
https://africatimes.com/2021/05/06/report-kenyas-wind-moroccos-solar-lead-africa-on-clean-energy/.

"Exterminate All the Brutes." HBO, April 19, 2021.
https://www.hbo.com/exterminate-all-the-brutes.

Hao, Karen. "Facebook's Ad Algorithms Are Still Excluding Women from Seeing Jobs." MIT Technology Review, June 17, 2021.
https://www.technologyreview.com/2021/04/09/1022217/facebook-ad-algorithm-sex-discrimination/.

History.com Editors. "Manifest Destiny." History.com, April 5, 2010.
https://www.history.com/topics/westward-expansion/manifest-destiny.

"India's Reliance Partners with Google, Facebook for Digital Payment Network Bid: ET." Reuters, February 27, 2021.
https://www.reuters.com/article/us-india-reliance-facebook-google/indias-reliance-partners-with-google-facebook-for-digital-payment-network-bid-et-idUSKBN2AR0CP.

Jacob Silverman. The New Republic. Accessed October 12, 2021.
https://newrepublic.com/authors/jacob-silverman.

"Jailed for a Facebook Post: How Us Police Target Critics with Arrest and Prosecution." The Guardian, May 18, 2017.
https://www.theguardian.com/us-news/2017/may/18/facebook-comments-arrest-prosecution.

Lizza, Ryan. "Americans Tune in to 'Cancel Culture' - and Don't Like What They See." POLITICO, July 27, 2020.
https://www.politico.com/news/2020/07/22/americans-cancel-culture-377412.

Mims, Christopher. "As Apple and Facebook Clash over Ads, Mom-and-Pop Shops Fear They'll Be the Victims." The Wall Street Journal, April 10, 2021.
https://www.wsj.com/articles/apple-facebook-clash-over-ads-small-businesses-fear-theyll-be-impacted-11618009627.

Nguyen, Viet Thanh. "The Sympathizer and The Committed: How the Model Minority Myth of Asian Americans Hurts Us All." Time, June 26, 2020.
https://time.com/5859206/anti-asian-racism-america/.

Nicas, Jack, and Katie Benner. "F.B.I. Asks Apple to Help Unlock Two IPhones." The New York Times, January 7, 2020.
https://www.nytimes.com/2020/01/07/technology/apple-fbi-iphone-encryption.html.

Raphael, Ray. *The U.S. Constitution: Explained—Clause by Clause—for Every American Today.* New York: Vintage Books, a division of Penguin Random House LLC, 2017.

Seely, Heather. "Investors Look toward the $330 Billion Green Finance Market." Blue and Green Tomorrow, October 12, 2021.
https://blueandgreentomorrow.com/invest/investors-look-toward-the-330-billion-green-finance-market/.

Service, Wire. "French Connection: Fear Stimulating Herd Instinct." Williams Lake Tribune, June 13, 2020.
https://www.wltribune.com/opinion/french-connection-fear-stimulating-herd-instinct/.

Sharma, Niharika. "Why the World Needs to Wake up to India's Jio." Quartz. Accessed October 12, 2021.
https://qz.com/india/1898734/with-facebook-google-ambanis-jio-can-be-a-global-tech-leader/.

Silverman, Jacob. "The Sad Implosion of Google's Ethical A.I." The New Republic, October 12, 2021.
https://newrepublic.com/article/161629/sad-implosion-googles-ethical-ai.

Singh, Manish. "Facebook Invests $5.7B in India's Reliance Jio Platforms." TechCrunch, April 22, 2020.
https://techcrunch.com/2020/04/21/facebook-reliance-jio/.

Singh, Manish. "Forget Winning, Can Amazon Survive in India?" TechCrunch, January 26, 2021.
https://techcrunch.com/2021/01/25/india-plays-hardball-with-amazon/.

"100 Years Later, What's The Legacy of 'Birth of a Nation'?" NPR, February 8, 2015. https://www.npr.org/sections/codeswitch/2015/02/08/383279630/100-years-later-whats-the-legacy-of-birth-of-a-nation.

"Three-Year Compliance Deadline for Kenya's Local Ownership." Capacity Media. Accessed October 12, 2021. https://www.capacitymedia.com/articles/3828256/three-year-compliance-deadline-set-for-kenyas-local-ownership-laws.

Tunkel, Anna, John Detrixhe. The NBER Digest. "Do the BRICS Need a Bigger Voice in the World?" World Economic Forum. Accessed October 12, 2021. https://www.weforum.org/agenda/2015/06/do-the-brics-need-a-bigger-voice-in-the-world/.

Walt, Vivienne. "Will India's Jio Be the Next Tech Giant?" Fortune, August 10, 2020. https://fortune.com/longform/jio-india-mukesh-ambani-tech-silicon-valley-facebook-alphabet-funding/.

CHAPTER 3

"5 Benefits of All-Electric, All-Digital Transformation." Financial Times, accessed October 12, 2021. https://www.ft.com/brandsuite/schneider-electric/5-benefits-of-digital-transformation-in-a-more-electric-world.html.

NAKAWEESI, DOROTHY. "Digital Stamps Have Exposed Dishonest Industrialists - Govt." Daily Monitor, December 17, 2020. https://www.monitor.co.ug/uganda/business/finance/digital-stamps-have-exposed-dishonest-industrialists-govt—3216106.

"China's New Digital Currency Is Easy to Use but You'll Be Watched." The Wall Street Journal, accessed October 12, 2021. https://www.wsj.com/video/china-new-digital-currency-is-easy-to-use-but-youll-be-watched/3CB7D4BF-FDD6-4240-9C9A-0B982953E81E.html.

"Episode 5: The Land of Our Fathers, Part 1." The New York Times, October 5, 2019. https://www.nytimes.com/2019/10/04/podcasts/1619-slavery-sugar-farm-land.html.

John, Mark. "Analysis - Defiant Rwanda Calls West's Bluff on Aid." Reuters, October 21, 2012. https://www.reuters.com/article/uk-rwanda-aid/analysis-defiant-rwanda-calls-wests-bluff-on-aid-idUKBRE89K03M20121021.

Quinlan, Ronald. "Investors Seek €395m from Sale of Stake in Facebook's Dublin 4 HQ." The Irish Times, September 7, 2021. https://www.irishtimes.com/business/commercial-property/investors-seek-395m-from-sale-of-stake-in-facebook-s-dublin-4-hq-1.4667203.

Richter, Felix. "Infographic: Nearly Half of Republicans Approve of Capitol Riot." Statista Infographics, January 8, 2021. https://www.statista.com/chart/23886/capitol-riot-approval/.

"Social Media Tax: Uganda Government Sued." CNN. Accessed October 12, 2021. https://www.cnn.com/2018/06/01/africa/uganda-social-media-tax/index.html.

CHAPTER 4

"An App That Pays You for Your Data? Yes, Actually." Marketplace. Accessed October 13, 2021.
https://www.marketplace.org/shows/marketplace-tech/an-app-that-pays-you-for-your-data-yes-actually/.

"Crypto's Overnight Sensation is Taking on the Web as We Know It." Bloomberg. Accessed October 13, 2021.
https://www.bloomberg.com/news/articles/2021-05-12/crypto-s-overnight-sensation-is-taking-on-the-web-as-we-know-it.

"Crypto's Overnight Sensation is Taking on the Web as We Know It." Bloomberg. Accessed October 13, 2021.
https://www.bloomberg.com/news/articles/2021-05-12/crypto-s-overnight-sensation-is-taking-on-the-web-as-we-know-it.

"Google Pledges $10 Billion to Strengthen U.S. Cybersecurity." Bloomberg. Accessed October 13, 2021.
https://www.bloomberg.com/news/videos/2021-08-25/google-pledges-10-billion-to-strengthen-u-s-cybersecurity-video.

Bloomberg Technology. Bloomberg.com. Accessed October 13, 2021.
https://www.bloomberg.com/technology.

"Deep Look into the WordPress Market Share (2019)." Kinsta®, January 19, 2021.
https://kinsta.com/wordpress-market-share/.

"Fact Sheet: Biden-Harris Administration Increases Lending to Small Businesses in Need, Announces Changes to PPP to Further Promote Equitable Access to Relief." The White House, February 22, 2021.
https://www.whitehouse.gov/briefing-room/statements-releases/2021/02/22/fact-sheet-biden-harris-administration-increases-lending-to-small-businesses-in-need-announces-changes-to-ppp-to-further-promote-equitable-access-to-relief/.

Ion, Florence. "Microsoft Kicks off Its Vision for a Password-Free Future." Gizmodo, September 15, 2021.
https://gizmodo.com/microsoft-kicks-off-its-vision-for-a-password-free-futu-1847681481.

Yellen, Janet. "America Is Strongest When We Engage with the World." Twitter, April 5, 2021.
https://twitter.com/SecYellen/status/1379095742082641921?s=20.

CHAPTER 5

Center, Electronic Privacy Information. "Epic - Data Protection Commissioner V. Facebook & Max Schrems (Irish High Court)." Electronic Privacy Information Center. Accessed October 13, 2021.
https://epic.org/privacy/intl/dpc-v-facebook/ireland/.

"Children's Privacy." Federal Trade Commission. Accessed October 13, 2021.
https://www.ftc.gov/tips-advice/business-center/privacy-and-security/children's-privacy.

"Children's Privacy." Federal Trade Commission. Accessed October 13, 2021.
https://www.ftc.gov/tips-advice/business-center/privacy-and-security/children's-privacy.

Console, Google Play. "Families: Google Play Console." Google Play Console. Accessed October 13, 2021.
https://developer.android.com/google-play/guides/families.

Diebner, Rachel, Elizabeth Silliman, Kelly Ungerman, and Maxence Vancauwenberghe. "Adapting Customer Experience in the Time of Coronavirus." McKinsey & Company, December 12, 2020.
https://www.mckinsey.com/business-functions/marketing-and-sales/our-insights/adapting-customer-experience-in-the-time-of-coronavirus.

"European Commission." European Commission. Accessed October 13, 2021.
https://ec.europa.eu/commission/priorities/justice-and-fundamental-rights/data-protection/2018-reform-eu-data-protection-rules_en#abouttheregulationanddataprotection.

"Facebook Loses Court Fight over Halting EU-US Data Transfers." Associated Press, May 14, 2021.
https://apnews.com/article/europe-data-privacy-technology-business-1f2550fcf3523df0706e1021a24bdd1f.

"Flutterwave Teams up with PayPal to Make It Easier for African Businesses to Accept and Make Payments." Business Insider. Accessed October 13, 2021.
https://africa.businessinsider.com/local/markets/flutterwave-teams-up-with-paypal-to-make-it-easier-for-african-businesses-to-accept/qj292qf.

Greim, Lisa. "Apple Slapped with Class Action Suit over in-App Purchases." Channel Daily News, April 18, 2011.
https://channeldailynews.com/news/apple-slapped-with-class-action-suit-over-in-app-purchases/17043.

"Home." African Union, November 15, 2021.
http://au.int/.

"International Dimension of Data Protection." European Commission, May 12, 2020.
https://ec.europa.eu/info/law/law-topic/data-protection/international-dimension-data-protection_en.

"YouTube Has a New App Just for Kids." CNNMoney. Accessed October 13, 2021.
https://money.cnn.com/2015/02/20/technology/mobile/youtube-for-kids/.

"The Last Digital Frontier." The Pear Dream Inc. Accessed October 13, 2021.
https://www.amazon.com/Last-Digital-Frontier-Technology-AskAsingia/dp/0578538571.

Nyairo, Daniel O. "M-Pesa Shuts down as Servers Move from Germany to Kenya." Cointelegraph, April 16, 2015.
https://cointelegraph.com/news/m-pesa-shuts-down-as-they-move-servers-from-germany-to-kenya.

Shapshak, Toby. "Vodacom and Safaricom Acquire M-Pesa to Accelerate Mobile Money Services in Africa." Forbes Magazine, April 6, 2020.
https://www.forbes.com/sites/tobyshapshak/2020/04/06/vodacom-and-safaricom-acquire-m-pesa-to-accelerate-mobile-money-services-in-africa/.

Silvia Amaro, Chloe Taylor. "Google Does Not Have to Apply 'Right to Be Forgotten' Globally, EU Court Rules." CNBC, September 24, 2019.
https://www.cnbc.com/2019/09/24/eu-rules-on-google-right-to-be-forgotten-case.html.

Silvia Amaro, Chloe Taylor. "Google Does Not Have to Apply 'Right to Be Forgotten' Globally, EU Court Rules." CNBC, September 24, 2019. https://www.cnbc.com/2019/09/24/eu-rules-on-google-right-to-be-forgotten-case.html.

"Sub-Saharan Africa: The Mobile Economy." GSMA, September 28, 2021. https://www.gsma.com/mobileeconomy/sub-saharan-africa/.

CHAPTER 6

"Agenda 2063: The Africa We Want." African Union, October 9, 2020. https://au.int/en/agenda2063/overview.

Ahmed, Yasmin. "Google India Announces New Features across Products to Help Users with Regional Languages." India Today, December 17, 2020. https://www.indiatoday.in/technology/news/story/google-india-announces-new-features-across-products-to-help-users-with-regional-languages-1750354-2020-12-17.

Baum, L. Frank, and Charles Santore. *The Wizard of Oz*. Kennebunkport: Cider Mill Press, 2021.

"China's Massive Belt and Road Initiative." Council on Foreign Relations. Accessed October 14, 2021. https://www.cfr.org/backgrounder/chinas-massive-belt-and-road-initiative.

Dollar, David. "Seven Years into China's Belt and Road." Brookings, October 1, 2020. https://www.brookings.edu/blog/order-from-chaos/2020/10/01/seven-years-into-chinas-belt-and-road/.

Goel, Vindu. "India Pushes Back against Tech 'Colonization' by Internet Giants." The New York Times, August 31, 2018. https://www.nytimes.com/2018/08/31/technology/india-technology-american-giants.html.

Kendall, Brent, and Tripp Mickle. "Google Wins Multibillion Dollar Copyright Fight with Oracle in Supreme Court." The Wall Street Journal, April 5, 2021. https://www.wsj.com/articles/supreme-court-rules-for-google-in-multibillion-dollar-copyright-battle-with-oracle-11617632233.

Kendall, Brent, and Tripp Mickle. "Google Wins Multibillion Dollar Copyright Fight with Oracle in Supreme Court." The Wall Street Journal, April 5, 2021. https://www.wsj.com/articles/supreme-court-rules-for-google-in-multibillion-dollar-copyright-battle-with-oracle-11617632233.

Langley, Noel, Florence Ryerson, Edgar Alan Woolf, Mervyn LeRoy, Herbert Stothart, E. Y. Harburg, Harold Arlen, dir. *The Wizard of Oz*. 1939; Warner Bros. Pictures, 1939. Blu-ray Disc, 1080p HD.

Liu, Alfred, Iain Marlow, and Bloomberg. "4 Hong Kong Opposition Lawmakers Ousted Minutes after Beijing Passes 'Patriot' Requirement." Fortune, November 11, 2020. https://fortune.com/2020/11/11/4-hong-kong-opposition-lawmakers-ousted-minutes-after-beijing-passes-patriot-requirement/.

Sharma, Shashi. "Only a Drunkard Would Accept These Terms: Tanzania President Cancels 'Killer Chinese Loan' Worth $10 Bn." IBTimes India, April 23, 2020. https://www.ibtimes.co.in/only-drunkard-would-accept-these-terms-tanzania-president-cancels-killer-chinese-loan-worth-10-818225.

Singh, Manish. "Ambani's Reliance Retail Raises $1.3 Billion from PIF." TechCrunch, November 5, 2020.
https://techcrunch.com/2020/11/05/reliance-retail-raises-1-3-billion-from-pif/.

Singh, Manish. "Forget Winning, Can Amazon Survive in India?" TechCrunch, January 26, 2021.
https://techcrunch.com/2021/01/25/india-plays-hardball-with-amazon/.

Singh, Manish. "In India, Amazon and Walmart Face off against the Country's Richest Man." VentureBeat, January 18, 2019.
https://venturebeat.com/2019/01/18/in-india-amazon-and-walmart-face-off-against-the-countrys-richest-man/.

Singh, Manish. "Indian Trader Group Calls for Ban on Amazon Following Damning Report." TechCrunch, February 17, 2021.
https://techcrunch.com/2021/02/17/indian-trader-group-calls-for-ban-on-amazon-following-dodging-regulations-claims/.

"South China Sea: What's China's Plan for Its 'Great Wall of Sand'?" BBC News, July 14, 2020.
https://www.bbc.com/news/world-asia-53344449.

CHAPTER 7

Wells, Myrydd. "Georgia Goes Blue for the First Time since 1992." Atlanta Magazine, November 13, 2020.
https://www.atlantamagazine.com/news-culture-articles/georgia-goes-blue-for-the-first-time-since-1992/.

Alderman, Liz, and David Gelles. "As Boeing Jets Sit Idle, Airbus Can't Make Planes Fast Enough." The New York Times, February 13, 2020.
https://www.nytimes.com/2020/02/13/business/airbus-boeing.html.

"Robinhood CEO Rebukes Critics in Call for Ubiquitous Investing." Bloomberg. Accessed October 14, 2021.
https://www.bloomberg.com/news/articles/2021-03-10/robinhood-ceo-rebukes-critics-in-call-for-ubiquitous-investing.

"Robinhood Gamestop Saga Pressures Payment for Order Flow." Bloomberg. Accessed October 15, 2021.
https://www.bloomberg.com/news/newsletters/2021-02-05/robinhood-gamestop-saga-pressures-payment-for-order-flow-kksjpbpt.

Pisani, Bob. "Robinhood-Gamestop Hearing Will Scrutinize How Brokerages Get Paid for Trades." CNBC, February 18, 2021.
https://www.cnbc.com/2021/02/18/payment-for-order-flow-the-controversial-wall-street-practice-to-draw-scrutiny-at-robinhood-hearing.html.

"Boeing CEO Fired: These Are the Mistakes That Cost Dennis…" CNN. Accessed October 15, 2021.
https://www.cnn.com/2019/12/24/business/boeing-dennis-muilenburg-mistakes/index.html.

"'Boeing Played Russian Roulette with People's Lives.'" BBC News. Accessed October 14, 2021.
https://www.bbc.co.uk/news/extra/jDOe2y9Tbo/boeing-737-max.

Booker, Brakkton, and David Schaper. "Boeing Chief to Families of Crash Victims: 'We Are Sorry, Deeply and Truly.'" NPR, October 29, 2019.
https://www.npr.org/2019/10/29/774345348/boeing-chief-to-families-of-crash-victims-we-are-sorry-deeply-and-truly.

Booker, Brakkton. "Trump Impeachment Trial Verdict: How Senators Voted." NPR, February 13, 2021.
https://www.npr.org/sections/trump-impeachment-trial-live-updates/2021/02/13/967539051/trump-impeachment-trial-verdict-how-senators-voted.

Campbell, Darryl. "Redline." The Verge, May 2, 2019.
https://www.theverge.com/2019/5/2/18518176/boeing-737-max-crash-problems-human-error-mcas-faa.

Cummings, Scott L. "The Lessons from Trump's 'Kraken' Lawyer Sanctions in Michigan." NBCNews.com, October 4, 2021.
https://www.nbcnews.com/think/opinion/lessons-trump-s-kraken-lawyer-sanctions-michigan-ncna1278188.

Egan, Matt, Brian Fung, and Clare Duffy. "Some Good Questions…" CNN, February 18, 2021.
https://www.cnn.com/business/live-news/robinhood-gamestop-reddit-hearing-congress/h_fbb497bf84eb82cd3ed3b57b7b7537e5.

Kitroeff, Natalie, and David Gelles. "Boeing C.E.O. Knew about Pilot's Warnings before Second Crash." The New York Times, October 29, 2019.
https://www.nytimes.com/2019/10/29/business/boeing-ceo-hearing.html.

Leggett, Theo. "Boeing's 737 MAX Aircraft under Scrutiny Again." BBC, May 10, 2021.
https://www.bbc.com/news/business-57028687.

"Let America Be America Again by Langston Hughes - Poems | Academy of American Poets." Academy of American Poets. Accessed October 15, 2021.
https://poets.org/poem/let-america-be-america-again.

"Meme Stocks Show That 'Community' Is Profitable: Reddit Co-Founder." Yahoo! Accessed October 15, 2021.
https://news.yahoo.com/meme-stocks-show-that-community-is-profitable-reddit-co-founder-173909883.html.

Newmyer, Tory, Douglas MacMillan, and Hamza Shaban. "Congress Presses Robinhood CEO on Company's Role in Gamestop Stock Frenzy." The Washington Post, February 19, 2021.
https://www.washingtonpost.com/business/2021/02/18/gamestop-robinhood-citadel-roaring-kitty-hearing-live-updates/.

Perrybaconjr. "How Georgia Turned Blue." FiveThirtyEight, November 18, 2020.
https://fivethirtyeight.com/features/how-georgia-turned-blue/.

Rudegeair, Peter, and AnnaMaria Andriotis. "WSJ News Exclusive | JPMorgan, Others Plan to Issue Credit Cards to People with No Credit Scores." The Wall Street Journal, May 13, 2021.
https://www.wsj.com/articles/jpmorgan-others-plan-to-issue-credit-cards-to-people-with-no-credit-scores-11620898206?mod=mhp.

Tangel, Andrew. "Boeing to Pay FAA Penalties Related to 737 Jet Production Problems." The Wall Street Journal, May 27, 2021.
https://www.wsj.com/articles/boeing-to-pay-faa-penalties-related-to-737-jet-production-problems-11622113200?mod=mhp.

Wires, News. "US Congress Grills Big Tech CEOS over Their Role in Fueling Misinformation, Capitol Siege." France 24, March 26, 2021.
https://www.france24.com/en/americas/20210326-us-congress-grills-big-tech-ceos-on-misinformation-capitol-siege.

X, Malcolm. "The Autobiography of Malcolm X: Paperback." Barnes & Noble, January 15, 1992.
https://www.barnesandnoble.com/w/autobiography-of-malcolm-x-malcolm-x/1002064844.

X., Malcolm, Alex Haley, and M. S. Handler. *The Autobiography of Malcolm X.* New York: Ballantine Books, 1992.

CHAPTER 8

Aten, Jason. "Apple and Facebook's Fight Isn't Actually about Privacy or Tracking. This Is the Real Reason Facebook Is so Worried." Inc., March 21, 2021.
https://www.inc.com/jason-aten/apple-facebooks-fight-isnt-about-privacy-or-tracking-real-reason-facebook-is-so-worried.html.

"Kenya's Biggest Bank Bets on Digital Payments for Growth." Bloomberg. Accessed October 15, 2021.
https://www.bloomberg.com/news/articles/2021-03-20/kenya-s-biggest-bank-bets-on-digital-payments-for-growth.

"Citizen 4." Edward Snowden. Accessed October 15, 2021.
https://edwardsnowden.com/.

Elias, Jenn. "Analysts Explain How the Apple-Epic Court Ruling Could Affect Google." CNBC, September 14, 2021.
https://www.cnbc.com/2021/09/13/how-the-apple-epic-court-ruling-could-affect-google-analysts.html.

Hill, Kashmir. "The Secretive Company That Might End Privacy as We Know It." The New York Times, January 18, 2020.
https://www.nytimes.com/2020/01/18/technology/clearview-privacy-facial-recognition.html.

Lawrence Lessig. *Code: Version 2.0.* Code Is Law. New York: SoHo Books, 2010.

Lyons, Kim. "Epic Has Appealed Friday's Ruling in the Epic v. Apple Case." The Verge, September 12, 2021.
https://www.theverge.com/2021/9/12/22670269/epic-files-appeal-fortnite-legal-battle.

"No Party Split in Views on Monitoring Allied Leaders' Calls." Pew Research Center, November 4, 2013.
https://www.pewresearch.org/politics/2013/11/04/most-say-monitoring-allied-leaders-calls-is-unacceptable/11-4-2013-2/.

Ovide, Shira. "Stay Safe from App Tracking." The New York Times, May 10, 2021.
https://www.nytimes.com/2021/05/10/technology/app-tracking.html.

"After Coupang Soars in US IPO, Can It Deliver for the Long Term?" Nikkei Asia, March 12, 2021.
https://asia.nikkei.com/Business/Business-Spotlight/After-Coupang-soars-in-US-IPO-can-it-deliver-for-the-long-term.

CHAPTER 9

"Google AI Researchers Lay Out Demands, Escalating Internal Fight." Bloomberg. Accessed October 16, 2021.
https://www.bloomberg.com/news/articles/2020-12-16/google-ai-researchers-lay-out-demands-escalating-internal-fight.

Bogost, Ian. "Apple's Empty Grandstanding about Privacy." The Atlantic, January 31, 2019.
https://www.theatlantic.com/technology/archive/2019/01/apples-hypocritical-defense-data-privacy/581680/.

Conger, Kate. "Google Removes 'Don't Be Evil' Clause from Its Code of Conduct." Gizmodo, May 18, 2018.
https://gizmodo.com/google-removes-nearly-all-mentions-of-dont-be-evil-from-1826153393.

Derousseau, Ryan. "We Want to Invest in ESG Funds, but Don't. Here's Why That's Okay (Based on Common Fire Investing Strategies)." Forbes Magazine, December 15, 2020.
https://www.forbes.com/sites/ryanderousseau/2019/08/28/we-want-to-invest-in-esg-funds-but-dont-heres-why-thats-okay-based-on-common-fire-investing-strategies/?sh=451b3e7c4eb3.

Apple. "Keynote Address from Tim Cook, CEO, Apple Inc." October 24, 2018. Video, 4:45.
https://www.youtube.com/watch?v=kVhOLkIs20A.

Feulner, Edwin. "The Cost of Doing the Right Thing." The Heritage Foundation. Accessed October 16, 2021.
https://www.heritage.org/health-care-reform/commentary/the-cost-doing-the-right-thing.

Harwell, Drew, and Nitasha Tiku. "Google's Star AI Ethics Researcher, One of a Few Black Women in the Field, Says She Was Fired for a Critical Email." The Washington Post, December 5, 2020.
https://www.washingtonpost.com/technology/2020/12/03/timnit-gebru-google-fired/.

Higgins, Tim, and Sarah E. Needleman. "In Apple Antitrust Trial, Judge Signals Interest in Railroad, Credit-Card Monopoly Cases." The Wall Street Journal, May 25, 2021.
https://www.wsj.com/articles/in-apple-antitrust-trial-judge-signals-interest-in-railroad-credit-card-monopoly-cases-11621940401?mod=hp_lista_pos2.

James Zou, Vineeta Agarwala, Euan Ashley and Hanne Winarsky, Vijay Pande Todd Park, and Malinka Walaliyadde Bill Frist. "Bio Eats World: The Trials of Clinical Trials." Andreessen Horowitz, May 25, 2021.
https://a16z.com/2021/05/18/bio-eats-world-the-trials-of-clinical-trials/.

Johnson, Khari. "Black Women, AI, and Overcoming Historical Patterns of Abuse." VentureBeat, April 10, 2021.
https://venturebeat.com/2021/04/10/black-women-ai-and-historical-patterns-of-abuse/.

London South Bank University. London South Bank University, July 6, 2021.
https://www.lsbu.ac.uk/.

Patricia Harned, Ph.D. "The Cost of 'Doing the Right Thing.'" HuffPost, March 20, 2012.
https://www.huffpost.com/entry/the-cost-of-doing-the-rig_b_1215717.

Priestley, Theo. "Apple Privacy May Not Be as Private as You Think." Forbes Magazine, August 24, 2015. https://www.forbes.com/sites/theopriestley/2015/08/24/did-apple-lie-about-your-privacy/?sh=2af532cc2b09.

O'Dea, S. "Mobile OS Market Share 2021." Statista, June 29, 2021. https://www.statista.com/statistics/272698/global-market-share-held-by-mobile-operating-systems-since-2009/.

Simonite, Tom. "What Really Happened When Google Ousted Timnit Gebru." Wired, June 8, 2021. https://www.wired.com/story/google-timnit-gebru-ai-what-really-happened/.

Smith, Rebecca. "After Colonial Pipeline Hack, U.S. to Require Operators to Report Cyberattacks." The Wall Street Journal, May 25, 2021. https://www.wsj.com/articles/tsa-to-require-pipeline-operators-to-notify-it-of-cyberattacks-11621960244?mod=hp_lead_pos7.

Tiku, Nitasha. "Google Hired Timnit Gebru to Be an Outspoken Critic of Unethical AI. Then She Was Fired for It." The Washington Post, December 30, 2020. https://www.washingtonpost.com/technology/2020/12/23/google-timnit-gebru-ai-ethics/.

Vincent, James. "Google Is Poisoning Its Reputation with AI Researchers." The Verge, April 13, 2021. https://www.theverge.com/2021/4/13/22370158/google-ai-ethics-timnit-gebru-margaret-mitchell-firing-reputation.

Zialcita, Paolo. "Facebook Pays $643,000 Fine for Role in Cambridge Analytica Scandal." NPR, October 30, 2019. https://www.npr.org/2019/10/30/774749376/facebook-pays-643-000-fine-for-role-in-cambridge-analytica-scandal.

CHAPTER 10

Abet, Felix Ainebyoona and Tonny. "Uganda: The Hidden Hands in Covidex Fights." allAfrica.com, July 19, 2021. https://allafrica.com/stories/202107190164.html.

"Addressing Global Health Inequities." Yale University. Accessed October 16, 2021. https://digitalcommons.law.yale.edu/cgi/viewcontent.cgi?article=4297&context=fss_papers.

"Apple Loses Trademark Fight over 'iPhone' Name in China." BBC, May 4, 2016. https://www.bbc.com/news/business-36200481.

Asingia, Brian. "Advisory, Consulting and Speaker Requests." DreamGalaxy Platform. Accessed October 16, 2021. http://www.brianasingia.com/.

Berger, Miriam. "Global Vaccine Inequality Runs Deep. Some Countries Say Intellectual Property Rights Are Part of the Problem." The Washington Post, February 23, 2021. https://www.washingtonpost.com/world/2021/02/20/poor-countries-arent-getting-vaccines-waiving-intellectual-property-rights-could-help/.

Blankenship, Mary, and Christina Golubski. "Nigeria's Twitter Ban Is a Misplaced Priority." Brookings, August 11, 2021. https://www.brookings.edu/blog/africa-in-focus/2021/08/11/nigerias-twitter-ban-is-a-misplaced-priority/.

"Jack Dorsey's Square Considers Building a Bitcoin Mining System." Bloomberg. Accessed October 17, 2021. https://www.bloomberg.com/news/articles/2021-10-15/jack-dorsey-s-square-considers-building-a-bitcoin-mining-system.

Browne, Ryan. "European Rival to PayPal and Square Makes $317 Million Acquisition to Expand in the U.S." CNBC, October 14, 2021. https://www.cnbc.com/2021/10/14/payments-firm-sumup-makes-317-million-acquisition-to-expand-in-us.html.

"Home." Home | African Union, October 14, 2021. http://www.au.int/.

Huizen, Jennifer. "Hard Choices: Ai in Health Care." Yale School of Medicine. Accessed October 17, 2021. https://app.getresponse.com/click.html?x=a62b&lc=SPVV0Y&mc=Ik&s=dL53Wj&u=wo5p6&z=EyAI2&.

"Madagascar's President Backs Herbal 'Cure' over Covid-19 Vaccines." South China Morning Post, March 21, 2021. https://www.scmp.com/news/world/africa/article/3126357/nothing-worry-about-madagascar-spurns-covid-19-vaccines-favour?module=perpetual_scroll&pgtype=article&campaign=3126357.

Olson, Parmy, and Betty Laura Zapata. "Four-Woman Group That Fought U.K. Algorithms Steps up for Tech-Worker Rights." The Wall Street Journal, May 15, 2021. https://www.wsj.com/articles/four-woman-group-that-fought-u-k-algorithms-steps-up-for-tech-worker-rights-11621087200?mod=mhp.

"Report to Congress Macroeconomic." Accessed October 17, 2021. https://home.treasury.gov/system/files/206/April_2021_FX_Report_FINAL.pdf.

Schechner, Sam. "Facebook Loses Bid to Block Ruling on EU-U.S. Data Flows." The Wall Street Journal, May 14, 2021. https://www.wsj.com/articles/facebook-faces-irish-ruling-on-suspension-of-eu-u-s-data-flows-11620983614?mod=mhp.

Schechner, Sam. "Facebook, Google Face 'Strong Pipeline' of Privacy Rulings in Europe." The Wall Street Journal, February 25, 2021. https://www.wsj.com/articles/facebook-google-face-strong-pipeline-of-privacy-rulings-in-europe-11614211200?mod=article_inline.

Schechner, Sam. "Tech Giants Face New Rules in Europe, Backed by Huge Fines." The Wall Street Journal, December 16, 2020. https://www.wsj.com/articles/tech-giants-face-new-rules-in-europe-backed-by-huge-fines-11608046500?mod=article_inline.

Szkutak, Rebecca. "Sequoia Leads $16 Million Series A Round into Verification Startup Middesk." Forbes Magazine, March 25, 2021. https://www.forbes.com/sites/rebeccaszkutak/2021/03/24/sequoia-leads-16-million-series-a-round-into-verification-startup-middesk/amp/.

"Viewpoint: Why Twitter Got It Wrong in Nigeria." BBC, August 14, 2021. https://www.bbc.com/news/world-africa-58175708.

"Why Is There No Aids Vaccine?" Brookings.edu. Accessed October 16, 2021. https://www.brookings.edu/wp-content/uploads/2016/06/20060720vaccine.pdf.

"WIPO - World Intellectual Property Organization." Accessed October 16, 2021. https://www.wipo.int/edocs/pubdocs/en/wipo_pub_1055_2021.pdf.

Yellen, Janet (@SecYellen). "America is strongest when we engage with the world. When I was born, the US was still recovering from the Depression & WWII. These tragedies cost countless lives; too many families lost everything. From the devastation, we learned an invaluable lesson: we must not go it alone. " Twitter, April 5, 2021. 10:37 AM. https://twitter.com/SecYellen/status/1379095742082641921?s=20.

CHAPTER 11

AfricaNews. "France and Rwanda Strengthen Relations, Increase Cooperation." Africanews, May 27, 2021. https://www.africanews.com/2021/05/27/france-and-rwanda-strengthen-relations-increase-cooperation//.

"Bill H.117 - Malegislature.gov." Accessed October 18, 2021. https://malegislature.gov/Bills/192/H117.

Buck-Morss, Susan. *Hegel, Haiti, and Universal History*. Pittsburgh PA: University OF PITTSBURGH Press, 2012.

"California County Sheriff Tried out Facial Recognition Tools." GovTech, April 20, 2021. https://app.getresponse.com/click.html?x=a62b&lc=SPVV9N&mc=Ik&s=dL53Wj&u=wo5p6&z=EMQMtl9&.

Computer Security Division, Information Technology Laboratory. "Explainable AI, Verification, and Validation - Combinatorial Testing: CSRC." CSRC. Accessed October 18, 2021. https://csrc.nist.gov/Projects/automated-combinatorial-testing-for-software/autonomous-systems-assurance/explainable-ai.

Data & Society. Accessed October 18, 2021. https://datasociety.net/.

France 24. "Replay: France's Macron Meets Rwanda's Kagame to Turn Page on Post-Genocide Tensions." May 27, 2021. https://www.youtube.com/watch?v=h8nflBltrL0.

Forrest, Brett. "China Says U.S. Blocked Joint U.N. Statement on Mideast." The Wall Street Journal, May 16, 2021. https://www.wsj.com/articles/china-says-u-s-blocked-joint-u-n-statement-on-mideast-11621199977?mod=mhp.

Johnson, Khari. "Incoming White House Science and Technology Leader on AI, Diversity, and Society." VentureBeat, January 16, 2021. https://app.getresponse.com/click.html?x=a62b&lc=SPVIg9&mc=Ik&s=dL53Wj&u=wo5p6&z=Et4Qw1F&.

Maruri, Katya. "Massachusetts Homes in on Facial Recognition Accountability." GovTech, May 20, 2021. https://www.govtech.com/policy/massachusetts-homes-in-on-facial-recognition-accountability.

OpenAI. OpenAI, June 18, 2021.
https://openai.com/.

"U.S. Senate Committee Revised a Draft Bill to Fund AI, Quantum, Biotech."
VentureBeat, May 8, 2021.
https://app.getresponse.com/click.
html?x=a62b&lc=SPVVBl&mc=Ik&s=dL53Wj&u=wo5p6&z=EzquzGR&.

"U.S. Senate Committee Revised a Draft Bill to Fund AI, Quantum, Biotech."
VentureBeat, May 8, 2021.
https://app.getresponse.com/click.
html?x=a62b&lc=SPVVBl&mc=Ik&s=dL53Wj&u=wo5p6&z=EzquzGR&.

United Bank of Africa. "UBA Africa Day 2021 (English) Africa to the World."
United Bank of Africa. May 25, 2021.
https://www.youtube.com/watch?v=XyY6mYx6ISM.

www.ingramcontent.com/pod-product-compliance
Lightning Source LLC
LaVergne TN
LVHW011830060526
838200LV00053B/3963